English for the Financial Sector

Student's Book

Ian MacKenzie

CAMBRIDGE
UNIVERSITY PRESS

CAMBRIDGE UNIVERSITY PRESS

Cambridge, New York, Melbourne, Madrid, Cape Town,
Singapore, São Paolo, Delhi, Tokyo, Mexico City

Cambridge University Press
The Edinburgh Building, Cambridge, CB2 8RU, UK

www.cambridge.org
Information on this title: www.cambridge.org/9780521547253

First published 2008
4th printing 2012

Printed in Dubai by Oriental Press

A catalogue record for this publication is available from the British Library

ISBN 978-0-521-54725-3 Student's Book
ISBN 978-0-521-54726-0 Teacher's Book
ISBN 978-0-521-54728-4 Audio CD

Thanks and acknowledgements

This book has been a long time in the making, so long that I need to thank no fewer than three long-suffering commissioning editors at CUP – Will Capel, Sally Searby and Chris Capper, without whom, etc. A very hands-on and hard-working editor and an inspired and meticulous copyeditor have also had a huge input into this course – Joy Godwin and Lyn Strutt. Five reviewers read early drafts and made lots of very useful suggestions – Hazel Allen, Susy Macqueen, Mike Reilly, Rosemary Richie and Alison Silver. Earlier still a number of people reviewed the original proposal: Ahmed Al-Tuhaini, Tim Banks, David Beesley, Fiona Dunbar, John Anthony Hall, Jessica Kou, Anthony Nicholson, Allen Santucci and Barry Siegel. My thanks go to all of the above, many of whom will willingly testify to my regular reluctance to accept very good advice.

Thanks are also due to Suzanne Williams of pictureresearch.co.uk for finding the photos, to Sophie Clarke, Michelle Simpson and Chris Willis at CUP, to Wild Apple Design for turning a drab manuscript into the attractive book you are holding, and to Sarah Hall for proofreading.

For the listening material I'd like to thank all the people who gave us their time and expertise (including some who did not make it to the final edit), particularly Peter Sinclair, Kate Barker, Gerlinde Igler, Rhys Roberts, Raymond Larcier and Aidan O'Connor. The recordings were produced and edited by Leon Chambers.

I would once again like to dedicate this book to Alex and Elliot, who wisely went to work in multilingual businesses, and to Charlotte, who wisely didn't!

The author and publishers would like to thank:

Peter Sinclair, Gerlinde Igler, Kate Barker and Professor Raymond Larcier for the interviews and photographs.

The author and publishers acknowledge the following sources of copyright material and are grateful for the permissions granted. While every effort has been made, it has not always been possible to identify the sources of all the material used, or to trace all copyright holders. If any omissions are brought to our notice, we will be happy to include the appropriate acknowledgements on reprinting.

p. 18: Hodder and Stoughton Limited and Michael Lewis for the front cover and extract from *Liar's Poker*, written by Michael Lewis. Reproduced by permission of Hodder and Stoughton Limited and Michael Lewis;

p. 20: *The Financial Times* for the article 'Banks to rely on branches to drive growth' by Jane Croft, 18 September 2002. Copyright © The Financial Times Limited;

p. 28: Global Investor for the logo and text 'Corporate Bonds' from www.finance-glossary.com. Reproduced by permission of Harriman House Ltd;

p. 38: Barclays Bank PLC for the Income Statement from the 2005 Annual Report/Annual Review and for p. 40 Consolidated balance sheet summary from the 2005 Annual Report/Annual Review. Copyright © 2005 Barclays Bank PLC. Reproduced by permission of Barclays Bank PLC;

p. 47: Bank of England for the text from the Bank of England website www.bankofengland.co.uk. Copyright © Bank of England;

p. 65: FX Trading from the website www.articlecity.com;

p. 71: *The New York Times* for the headline 'Stocks plunge 508 points, a drop of 22.6%', *The New York Times* 20 October 1987. All rights reserved. Used by permission and protected by the Copyright Laws of the United States. The printing, copying, redistribution, or transmission of the Material without express written permission is prohibited;

p. 72: *BBC News Online* for 'Why stock markets matter for you' by Stefan Armbruster and for p. 91 'Buffett warns on investment time bomb'. Copyright © BBC News Online, bbc.co.uk;

p. 85: *The Art of Business: Learn to Love Negotiating*, from the website: www.creativepro.com;

p. 99: *The Economist* for the article 'Fund management: Mug's game', 31 August 2002. Copyright © The Economist Newspaper Limited.

We would like to thank the following for permission to reproduce copyright photographs and cartoons:

Action Plus p 10 (Neil Tingle); Alamy pp 75 (Michael Jones), 77 (View Pictures Ltd), 83 (Blinkstock); Cartoonbank.com pp 15 © The New Yorker Collection 1993 Robert Mankoff from Cartoonbank.com All Rights Reserved, 17 © The New Yorker Collection 1999 Charles Barsotti from Cartoonbank.com All Rights Reserved, 28 © The New Yorker Collection 2007 Robert Mankoff from Cartoonbank.com All Rights Reserved, 95 © The New Yorker Collection 2001 Charles Barsotti from Cartoonbank.com All Rights Reserved, 98 © The New Yorker Collection 1997 Mike Twohy from Cartoonbank.com All Rights Reserved, 110 © The New Yorker Collection 2002 Tom Cheney from Cartoonbank.com All Rights Reserved; Cartoonstock. com pp 23 (Jerry King), 27 (Jerry King), 79 (Joseph Farris); Sophie Clarke p 96; Corbis pp 33 (James Nazz), 44 (Christine Schneider/zefa), 52 (Jagadeesh/Reuters), 57 (Hapag-Lloyd/epa), 71 (Bettmann), 89 (John Gress), 111 (Deepak Buddhiraja/India Picture); Getty Images pp 37 (Longview/Taxi), 63 (Micheal Simpson), 107 (Thomas Northcut); Reproduced by kind permission of Ted Goff/www.newslettercartoons.com pp 81, 84; Reproduced by kind permission of PRIVATE EYE pp 53 (Steve Way), 101 (Martin Honeysett); Punchstock pp 41 (Comstock Images), 46 (Andrew Ward/Life File/Photodisc), 97 (Comstock Images); Reuters p 62 (Sherwin Crasto); Rex Features p 21 (Sutton-Hibbert); UPS p 109 (DOONESBURY ©2002 G. B. Trudeau/Reprinted with permission of UNIVERSAL PRESS SYNDICATE All rights reserved).

Illustration on p88 by Andy Parker.

Contents

Introduction

English for the Financial Sector is a course for business students and people working in the financial industry with an intermediate or upper-intermediate level of English.

The course **aims** to:
- explain the basic concepts of most areas of finance
- build your financial vocabulary through reading, listening and discussion
- develop your comprehension of financial texts
- develop your listening skills in financial English
- improve your speaking skills through discussion, case studies and role plays
- develop your business communication proficiency by increasing your confidence and fluency in a range of skills
- practise specific language functions such as advising, suggesting, agreeing and disagreeing, clarifying, reviewing, and summarizing.

The course consists of **24 units**.

The **odd-numbered units** cover a particular area of finance, such as retail banking, investment banking, trade finance, asset management and accounting. They include authentic interviews with people working in finance, authentic business reading texts, and comprehension, vocabulary and discussion activities.

The **even-numbered units** practise business communication skills – telephoning, socializing, participating in meetings, writing letters, emails and reports, negotiating, and making presentations – in a financial context.

Each unit has a **Language focus** section looking at a specific language area and **Practice** activities using realistic situations from the financial industry.

The listening material includes British, American, European and Indian speakers. Tapescripts of all the listening material are included at the end of the book.

If you are still studying business or finance, you may learn new financial concepts from this book. If you are already working in finance, you will be able to use your knowledge and experience in the activities and exercises in this course.

You will probably be using this book in a class with a teacher. If so, try to participate as much as possible in the pair work and group activities, as this will increase the time you spend practising speaking, and so improve your fluency and confidence.

I hope you enjoy using this book.

1 The organization of the financial industry

AIMS

To learn about: the organization of the financial industry; key vocabulary of banking products and services
To learn how to: express permission, necessity and prohibition
To practise: asking and talking about terms and conditions of bank accounts

Lead in

- What services does your bank offer? Which of them do you use?
- If you are still studying, what area of finance do you want to work in, and why?
- If you are already working, what area of finance do you work in, and why? Would you like to change your field of activity in the future, and why?
- Has the institution or company you work for changed significantly in recent years? In what ways?

Vocabulary 1

You are going to listen to Peter Sinclair, the former director of the Centre for Central Banking Studies at the Bank of England, talking about the financial industry. Before you listen, check your understanding of banking vocabulary by completing each sentence with a word from the box.

bonds	deposit	mortgage	shares	takeover
capital	merger	pension	stocks	

1 A _____ is a loan to buy property.
2 Money you put in the bank is called a _____.
3 Money paid to a retired person is called a _____.
4 Securities representing part-ownership of a company are called _____ or
   _____.
5 The money invested in a business is its _____.
6 _____ are interest-paying securities issued by companies that need to borrow money.
7 A _____ is when a company gains control of another one by buying its stocks.
8 A _____ is when two formerly separate companies join together.

Listening 1: The development of the financial industry

Listen to Peter Sinclair talking about the organization of the financial industry 25 years ago, and answer the questions below. **1.1**

1 Were most financial institutions national, or international?
2 Were most financial institutions specialized, or did they offer lots of services?

3 What kinds of financial institutions traditionally did the following types of business? Complete the table.

making loans   issuing shares or bonds
arranging mergers   arranging mortgages
providing pensions   arranging or fighting takeover bids
giving financial advice to companies offering life insurance
receiving deposits

Retail banks	
Building societies	
Insurance companies	
Investment banks	

Listening 2: Going international

Listen to Peter Sinclair talking about recent changes in the financial industry, and answer the questions below. **1.2**

1 What has recently happened to banks in Britain and many other countries?
2 In what way does Peter Sinclair compare the City of London to the Wimbledon tennis tournament?
3 Which two words does Peter Sinclair use to summarize the two big recent trends in banking?

Peter Sinclair makes a comparison between the City of London and the Wimbledon tennis tournament.

Discussion

Has your bank changed in any of the ways described by Peter Sinclair?

Vocabulary 2

1 You are going to read about changes in the banking industry. Before you read, check your understanding of the words (1–8) below by matching them with their definitions (a–h).

1	conglomerates	a	abolished or ended rules and restrictions
2	depositors	b	sums of money paid as penalties for breaking the law
3	deregulated	c	groups of companies that have joined together
4	fines	d	control of something by rules or laws
5	prohibited	e	guaranteeing to buy a company's newly issued stocks if no one else does
6	regulation	f	made it illegal to do something
7	repealed	g	people who place money in bank accounts
8	underwriting	h	cancelled or ended (a law)

2 Now look again at the words above and put a stress mark in front of the stressed syllable in each word.
Example: con'glomerates

Reading: Regulation and deregulation

1 Read the article, and complete it using the words (1–8) from the **Vocabulary** exercise above.

Regulation and deregulation

In the late 1920s, several American commercial banks that were (1) _____ security issues for companies weren't able to sell the stocks to the public, because there wasn't enough demand. So they used money belonging to their (2) _____ to buy these securities. If the stock price later fell, their customers lost a lot of money.

This led the government to step up the (3) _____ of banks, to protect depositors' funds, and to maintain investors' confidence in the banking system. In 1933 the Glass–Steagall Act was passed, which (4) _____ American commercial banks from underwriting securities. Only investment banks could issue stocks for corporations. In Britain too, retail or commercial banks remained separate from investment or merchant banks. A similar law was passed in Japan after World War II.

Half a century later, in the 1980s and 90s, many banks were looking for new markets and higher profits in a period of increasing globalization. So most industrialized countries (5) _____ their financial systems. The Glass–Steagall Act was

(6) _____. A lot of commercial banks merged with or acquired investment banks and insurance companies, which created large financial (7) _____. The larger American and British banks now offer customers a complete range of financial services, as the universal banks in Germany and Switzerland have done for a long time. The law forbidding US commercial banks from operating in more than one state was also abolished. In Britain, many building societies, which specialized in mortgages, started to offer the same services as commercial banks.

Yet in all countries, financial institutions are still quite strictly controlled, either by the central bank or another financial authority. In 2002, ten of Wall Street's biggest banks paid (8) _____ of $1.4 billion for having advised investors, in the 1990s, to buy stocks in companies that they knew had financial difficulties. They had done this in order to get investment banking business from these companies – exactly the kind of practice that led the US government to separate commercial and investment banking in the 1930s.

2 Put the sentences (a–d) below in the right order on the timeline, and write the time period that each sentence refers to. The first one has been done as an example.

    a   Major US banks were fined for giving bad advice to investors.
    b   Commercial banks used their investors' money to buy securities and many depositors lost money.
    c   Many banking regulations were ended and big financial conglomerates were formed.
    d   New laws in the US and Britain separated commercial and investment banks.

1900   *b – 1920s*   2000

3 Look at the following statements. Are they true or false, according to the article?

    1   The Glass–Steagall Act was the result of the behaviour of investment banks.
    2   The British and American financial markets are now completely unregulated.
    3   German and Swiss banks did all types of banking business at a time when American and British ones were not allowed to.
    4   During the 20th century, many financial markets first became more regulated, and then less regulated.
    5   Large American banks no longer do the kind of things that led to the separation of investment and commercial banking in the 1930s.

Discussion

- Which are the largest banks (or financial conglomerates) in your country?
- To what extent is banking regulated in your country? What are the advantages and disadvantages of this?

Permission, necessity and prohibition

1 The **Reading** article gives information about banking regulations – how banking is controlled by rules. Look at the following sentences and underline the words that are used to describe things that are permitted, necessary, not necessary, or prohibited (forbidden).

    1   Although banks are allowed to open on Saturdays, most of them don't.
    2   Banks aren't allowed to charge less than the minimum interest rate.
    3   Commercial banks have to deposit part of their reserves at the central bank.
    4   If you have a credit card, you don't need to pay cash.
    5   If you keep at least $1,000 in the bank, you don't have to pay charges.
    6   Today, retail banks need to react to competition from building societies.
    7   Our policy states that we can't lend you more than one month's salary.
    8   You can pay me back at the end of the month.
    9   You must keep at least $1,000 in the account if you want free banking.
   10   You mustn't use this loan for any other purpose.
   11   You needn't go to the bank – you can do it on the internet.

2 Put the sentences into the correct columns, according to their meaning. The first one has been done as an example.

Meaning	Permission	Necessity or obligation	No necessity or no obligation	Prohibition
Sentence number	1			
Verbs used	*be allowed to*			

These verbs change if we talk about the past:

Present	Past
can / can't	was / were (not) able to OR could / couldn't
must	had to
mustn't	was / were not allowed to OR couldn't
is / are (not) allowed to	was / were (not) allowed to OR could / couldn't
has / have to	had to
doesn't / don't have to	didn't have to
need to	needed to
needn't / don't need to	didn't need to

Examples: I had a credit card, so I *didn't need to* pay cash.
          I *had to* keep $1,000 in the account.

3 Complete each sentence using a verb. Look back at the **Reading** and **Listening** exercises to find the information you need.

1 In the 1970s, US commercial banks _____ do business in more than one state.
2 Today, US banks _____ operate in several states.
3 Today, American banks _____ be specialized any more.
4 For most of the 20th century, commercial banks _____ issue shares.
5 Banks _____ sell stocks to their own customers if it is not in the customers' interest.
6 Today, building societies _____ restrict their activity to mortgages.
7 German banks were always _____ do business with both large companies and small individual customers.
8 Before deregulation, foreign banks _____ operate in many countries.
9 Even after deregulation, banks still _____ obey a lot of laws.
10 Twenty-five years ago, most banks _____ worry about foreign competition.

Practice

A customer calls a bank to ask about the terms and conditions of a bank account. Your teacher will give you a role to prepare. Use the phrases for permission, necessity and prohibition from the **Language focus** above.

Work in pairs. Student A should look at **page 115**, and Student B at **page 123**.

Discussion

How do the bank accounts in the **Practice** compare with your own? Talk about the rules for your account using the language from the **Language focus** above.

2 Telephoning

To learn how to: handle information and make arrangements on the telephone

To practise: asking for and giving information and arranging meetings on the telephone

Lead in

- What are the main differences between speaking on the phone and face-to-face?
- What do you find difficult about using the telephone in English?
- Do you prefer making telephone calls or writing emails? Why?

Listening 1: Arranging meetings

1 You are going to listen to two telephone calls between colleagues arranging a meeting. There are a number of stages in arranging a meeting on the phone. Before you listen, think of phrases that can be used at each stage.

1 Ask for a meeting:	5 Suggest another day or time:
2 Suggest a day:	6 Say that a day or time is possible:
3 Suggest a time:	7 Arrange the place:
4 Say that a day or time is not possible:	8 Confirm the arrangement:

2 Now listen to two short calls, and add the phrases the callers use at each stage to the table opposite. 🔘 **2.1**

3 Are the phrases they use formal or informal?

4 Match the two parts to make more phrases for arranging a meeting. Then add the phrases to the table opposite.

1	Is Friday	a	would be fine.
2	Can we	b	we meet here?
3	Where shall we	c	arrange a meeting?
4	Yes of course. Let me	d	have the meeting?
5	Can we fix a time	e	good for you?
6	Would Thursday	f	a meeting next week?
7	Why don't	g	seeing you next week.
8	I look forward to	h	check my diary.
9	OK, Thursday	i	be convenient for you?
10	Can we have	j	to meet?

Practice 1

Four bank employees have been taking part in a conference call, and are now trying to arrange a meeting for the following morning. Your teacher will give you a role to prepare. Use the phrases for arranging meetings from **Listening 1** and the exercises above.

Work in groups of four. Student A should look at **page 115**, Student B at **page 123**, Student C at **page 134**, and Student D at **page 132**.

MANKOFF

"No, Thursday's out. How about never – is never good for you?"

LANGUAGE FOCUS

Pronouncing the alphabet and saying telephone numbers

If you have to spell something, it's important to pronounce the letters clearly. The letters in the table below are grouped according to their vowel sound, shown at the top of the column.

Vowel sound	/eɪ/	/iː/	/e/	/uː/	/aɪ/	/ɑː/	/əʊ/
	A H J K	B C D E G P T V Z*	F L M N S X Z*	Q U W	I Y	R	O

★ Z is pronounced *zee* in American English and *zed* in British English.

When we read long strings of numbers, such as telephone numbers, passport numbers, credit card numbers, and car registration numbers, we usually say each digit separately.

Example:
You can phone him on 001 202 456 1414.

British English: *oh oh one, two oh two, four five six, one four one four*
American English: *zero zero one, two zero two, four five six, one four one four*

An exception to this is 'double numbers':

944 2299   *nine double four, double two double nine*
944 2229   *nine double four, double two two nine*

However, we do <u>not</u> usually say *double oh* or *double zero* at the beginning of an international number.

When saying numbers, we use a rising intonation for every group of numbers except the last one, when we use a falling tone. This shows we have reached the end of the number.

Example:

   ↗   ↗   ↗   ↘

  0044   223   325   844

Read the following sentences out loud:

1 My home number is 0044 207 270 1234.
2 And my fax is 207 925 0918.
3 Call me on my mobile: 087 966 3402.
4 The winning lottery ticket was QY 299 664 532 – and mine was QY 299 664 533.
5 His car number plate is AZ 314 586.

Listening 2: Handling information

1 Listen to the conversation between a customer and a customer service advisor in a bank. The customer is asking for information about loans. Complete the form below. ◎ **2.2**

Caller's name:	....
Subject of call:	....
Amount of loan:	....
Type of loan:	....
How loan is to be secured:	....
	....
Possible repayment options:	....
	....
Caller's phone number:	....

2 Now listen again and make a note of the language used in the call.  2.2

1 What the customer says to explain why he's calling:

_____

2 How the customer service advisor asks what information the customer needs:

_____

3 Two phrases the customer uses to ask for information:

_____

_____

4 What the customer service advisor asks to get more precise information:

_____

5 How the customer service advisor asks for the customer's name:

_____

Useful phrases

You will probably recognize some of the typical telephone phrases below, even with their
words in the wrong order. Rewrite them correctly, adding capital letters and punctuation
where needed.

1 repeat please you could that

_____

2 that do you how spell

_____

3 say you did sorry ...

_____

4 again over go that sorry we could

_____

5 back read can to you that I

_____

Practice 2

A student calls a company to ask for information
about a Graduate Training Programme. Your teacher
will give you a role to prepare. Use the phrases for
handling information from **Listening 2** above.

Work in pairs. Student A should look at **page 115**, and
Student B at **page 124**.

"*Eat your lunch, and then we'll see about giving your phone back.*"

3 Retail banking

AIMS

To learn about: developments in retail banking, banking products and services; key vocabulary of retail banking
To learn how to: express likelihood and probability
To practise: talking about the future of retail banking

Lead in

- What services would you expect a retail or commercial bank to offer?
- What is the difference between retail banking and investment banking?
- How do commercial banks make money?

Reading 1: Commercial and investment banking

1 *Liar's Poker* is Michael Lewis's very funny book about working as an investment banker in New York and London. In this extract, he explains why he didn't want to become a commercial or retail banker. Read the text and explain in your own words what Lewis is saying about:

1 commercial bankers
2 investment bankers.

> ... in 1934, American lawmakers had stripped investment banking out from commercial banking. Investment bankers now underwrote securities, such as stocks and bonds. Commercial bankers, like Citibank, took deposits and made loans. ... After Glass–Steagall most people became investment bankers. Now I didn't actually know any commercial bankers, but a commercial banker was reputed to be just an ordinary American businessman with ordinary American ambitions. He lent a few hundred million dollars each day to South American countries. But really,
>
> he meant no harm. He was only doing what he was told to do by someone higher up in an endless chain of command. ... He had a wife, a station wagon, 2.2 children, and a dog that brought him his slippers when he returned home from work at six. ... An investment banker was a breed apart, a member of a master race of deal makers. He possessed vast, almost unimaginable, talent and ambition. If he had a dog it snarled. He had two little red sports cars yet wanted four. To get them, he was, for a man in a suit, surprisingly willing to cause trouble.

2 Find words or phrases in the text that mean the following:

1 to separate
2 generally considered to be
3 didn't want to cause trouble for other people
4 a big hierarchy of directors and managers
5 special; different from other people
6 extremely big

3 'He lent a few hundred million dollars each day to South American countries.' This is an exaggeration. What other exaggerations or jokes can you find in the text?

Discussion

Which area would you prefer to work in – commercial banking or investment banking? Why?

Vocabulary 1

You are going to listen to Peter Sinclair, who we heard in **Unit 1**, talking about retail banking. Before you listen, check your understanding of the words and phrases in the box by matching them with their definitions (1–7).

assets	income	national income	trend
currency	lucrative	liabilities	

1 a general development or change in a situation or in people's behaviour
2 all the money received by a person during a particular period
3 anything of value owned by a business; for a bank, the loans it has made
4 money that a company will have to pay to someone else one day; for a bank, its deposits
5 profitable (describes an activity that makes a profit)
6 the money earned by a country's people in a particular period
7 the money used in a particular country

Listening: Retail banking

1 Listen to Peter Sinclair talking about retail banking. According to what he says, is retail banking in decline? *3*

2 Listen again and look at the following statements. Are they true or false, according to Peter Sinclair? *3*

   1 In the past, people used to keep more money in cash.
   2 Because of retail banks, national income is increasing in developing countries.
   3 Some people think that investment banking is more exciting than retail banking.
   4 Investment banking is more profitable than retail banking.
   5 There is more risk involved in investment banking than retail banking.

Discussion

   • How has commercial or retail banking changed since the 1980s?
   • How do you think it will develop in the next few years?

Vocabulary 2

1 Read the web page below advertising online banking, and complete the sentences overleaf.

Why bank online?

Because you have access to your account 24 hours a day, 7 days a week.
With internet banking you can:

   • Check your balance whenever you want.
   • Pay bills without writing cheques or queuing at the bank.
   • Transfer money between your current account and your savings account.
   • Print a statement at any time.
   • Set up, change and delete your standing orders.
   • View and cancel direct debits.
   • Apply for a loan.
   • Apply for a new or increased overdraft.
   • Order foreign currency or traveller's cheques.

1 A _____ _____ is an instruction to a bank to pay varying sums of money to another account on particular dates.

2 A _____ _____ pays interest but usually has limits as to how much money can be withdrawn during a certain period of time.

3 A _____ lists the recent debits and credits in a bank account.

4 An _____ is an arrangement allowing someone to borrow money by withdrawing more than they have deposited in their account, up to a certain limit.

5 A _____ _____ pays no or little interest, but usually allows the holder to withdraw cash or pay cheques without any restrictions.

6 A _____ is an amount of money borrowed from a bank for a fixed period.

7 A _____ is the amount of money in a bank account at a particular time.

8 A _____ _____ is an instruction to a bank to pay regular, fixed sums of money to another account.

2 Use a word or phrase from each box to make common word combinations. You can use some words more than once.

apply for	the balance
cancel	a cheque
check	an overdraft
set up	a direct debit
transfer	a loan
write	money
	a standing order

Reading 2: The future of bank branches

1 Read the article about retail banking from the *Financial Times*. What belief does the research show to be untrue?

Banks to rely on branches to drive growth

By Jane Croft

Banks will rely on branches to drive future growth rather than the internet, according to new research.

A study of 2,709 customers by Deloitte & Touche, the professional services firm, showed that the bank branch is the preferred channel for 52 per cent of customers interviewed.

Only 16 per cent preferred to bank using the telephone and 8 per cent used the internet.

The study also showed that the bank branch is preferred by 45 per cent of customers in the affluent AB social group – contradicting the notion that sophisticated customers avoid branches.

Nick Sandall, retail financial services partner at Deloitte & Touche, said he believed that the main banks in the UK were planning to reverse a decade of under-investment in branches by putting the network at the heart of their strategy.

'Although some banks, such as Abbey National, are ahead of the game in their efforts to revolutionise the way in which they use branches to reach the consumer, we expect all banks to invest substantially in reshaping their branch networks and the activities within,' he said.

Deloitte & Touche believed that the successful retail bank of the future needed to give careful consideration to areas such as branch design, staffing and location.

Abbey National, which has introduced Costa coffee shops into some of its branches, reports that banking product sales have increased in these locations.

2 Which of the highlighted words and phrases in the article could be replaced with the following?

1 decisions on types and numbers of employees
2 in advance of competitors
3 make business increase in the years to come
4 redesigning
5 spend a lot of money on
6 ten years of insufficient spending
7 wealthy

3 Read the article again and answer the following questions.

1 What have the banks not done during the past ten years?
2 What are banks expected to do in the future?
3 What has helped one bank to increase product sales in some branches?

4 Label the pie chart below.

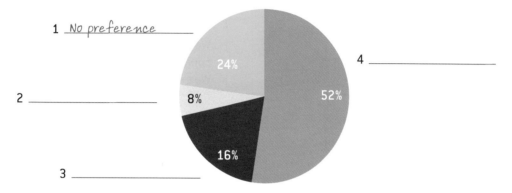

1 *No preference*

2 _____

3 _____

4 _____

24%

8%

52%

16%

Discussion

- Think about a bank's different delivery channels, or the different ways of banking. What are the relative advantages and disadvantages of these for the customer?
- Which types of customers are likely to prefer which delivery channels?
- What are the relative benefits and disadvantages of the different channels for the bank?
- Which way of banking do you prefer, and why? What services do you expect from a bank?

LANGUAGE FOCUS

Likelihood and probability

1 In the **Financial Times** article, there are some predictions about retail banking trends in the future. Look at the following sentences, which use phrases to show likelihood and probability. Put the sentences (a–l) on the scale (1–5), and underline the word or phrase that states the probability. One sentence has been done as an example.

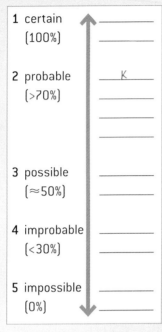

1 certain (100%)	_____
	_____
2 probable (>70%)	K
	_____
	_____
	_____
3 possible (≈50%)	_____
	_____
4 improbable (<30%)	_____
	_____
5 impossible (0%)	_____
	_____

a   E-banking is unlikely to decrease over the next 10 years.
b   I may well decide to change banks.
c   Interest rates can't possibly stay so low.
d   There could be a takeover, but I think it's improbable.
e   Our profits will definitely increase this year.
f   Perhaps we need to hire more financial advisors.
g   Small regional banks are bound to join together.
h   They'll probably move their call centre to India.
i   Universal banks are likely to spread.
j   We certainly won't reduce the size of our counselling area.
k   We <u>expect</u> all banks <u>to</u> invest substantially in their branch networks.
l   We might increase our commission charges.

2 Can you think of any other phrases we can use for describing likelihood and probability?

Discussion

In pairs, use some of the phrases from the **Language focus** above to make some predictions about the future of:

telephone banking
internet banking
branch banking
small national and regional banks
universal banking

the stock market in your country
interest rates in your country
your language learning
your company
your career

Example:
I *may well* go to the UK for an intensive language course next year.

Practice

MGS Bank has to decide whether to invest substantially in its 30 branches, or whether to try to encourage its customers to use the telephone and the internet. The Head of Retail Operations and the Head of Internet Banking have a meeting with the Chief Operating Officer to discuss this, before the Board meeting next week. Your teacher will give you a role to prepare. Use the phrases for expressing probability from the **Language focus** above.

Work in groups of three. Student A should look at **page 115**, Student B at **page 124**, and Student C at **page 134**.

4 Business correspondence 1

To learn how to: write emails using standard phrases; use formal and informal style

To practise: writing business emails; saying email and web addresses

Lead in

- What are the advantages and disadvantages of email?
- In what situations would you write an email rather than make a telephone call?

Discussion

Which of the statements below do you agree with?

"I've located the source of all that annoying spam we've been receiving...preparing to destroy."

EMAIL ETIQUETTE

1 Clearly summarize the contents of your message in the subject line, e.g. write 'May 23 Project Management Team Meeting Agenda' rather than just 'Meeting'.

2 Don't use the Cc (carbon copy) function to copy your message to everyone unless you really need to.

3 Use Bccs (blind carbon copies) when sending a message to a large group of people who don't know each other.

4 If you normally address a person as Ms / Mrs / Mr ___ , then that's what you do in a first email; if you normally call them by their first name, then you do that.

5 Reply to a message, don't start a new email. Keep the 'thread' by leaving the original messages attached.

6 Keep your messages shorter than a page, so readers don't have to scroll. People reading messages on cell phones and mobile devices often ignore long messages.

7 If you need someone to give you information or do something for you, be very specific.

8 To communicate very complex information, use the telephone, or face-to-face conversation, rather than email.

9 AVOID CAPITAL LETTERS – THEY'RE THE EQUIVALENT OF SHOUTING IN SOMEONE'S EAR AND THEY'RE MORE DIFFICULT TO READ.

10 Use capitalization and punctuation the same way that you would in any other document. Don't over-use exclamation marks!!!!!!

11 Smileys are used in personal emails and are not appropriate for business ;-)

12 There is no such thing as a private email. The system administrator can probably read all mails, and anyone can easily forward your message, even accidentally.

13 Somewhere in the world there is a hacker who can read your mail if he tries hard enough.

14 Don't write anything you wouldn't say to a person's face or in public or write on the back of a postcard.

15 If you send it from the office, it comes from the office: personal emails sent from work are regarded as official company communications, whatever their content.

16 Use the spel chek and re-read you mesage one last time before yoo send it.

Formal and informal style 1

when people write emails 2 friends they often use a v informal style. they dont worry much about speling, using capital letters using correct grammer writing in paragraphs punctuation and so on. sometimes they use abbrevs like in txt messages. U definitely shouldnt do this when writing bizness emails

1 Rewrite the email above in correct standard English.

Formal and informal words and phrases

A first email to someone in another company is usually quite formal, like a business letter (see **Unit 6**), but later emails often become more informal. Internal communication between colleagues is also usually relatively informal.

English often has a short word of Germanic origin and a longer word of Latin or French origin that means nearly the same thing. We use the longer words in more formal situations.

2 Match each of the short words (1–6) to one of the longer words (a–f) with a similar meaning.

1	ask	a	commence
2	begin	b	obtain
3	buy	c	enquire
4	get	d	inform
5	give	e	purchase
6	tell	f	provide

Most phrasal verbs also have a one-word Latinate equivalent, which is more formal.

Examples:
  We are going to *bring in | implement* new accounting policies.
  You need to *look into | investigate* these claims.
  They are trying to *get rid of | eradicate* their debts.

Leaving out words

Although spelling and punctuation should usually be correct – an email is <u>not</u> a text message – emails between friends and colleagues are sometimes written like telegrams used to be, with unnecessary words left out. The full grammatical form is not necessary if the meaning is clear from the context.

People also often use acronyms (the first letters of words) such as *TIA* (thanks in advance), *asap* (as soon as possible), *FYI* (for your information), *BTW* (by the way) and *BW* (best wishes). In informal emails, people writing quickly often use short forms of common words: *yr, pls, thx* or *thnx, rgds, re* (your, please, thanks, regards, with reference to). It's worth remembering that using acronyms and short forms might be considered unprofessional in some business situations, especially when you do not know the person you are writing to very well.

3 Match the sentences (1–10) to the descriptions (a–e). One of the sentences can be matched to two descriptions.

1 Flying via New York (would be) quicker.
2 (I'll) Speak to you later.
3 (It's a) Shame you can't come.
4 Their plans (are) uncertain.
5 (Are you) Coming to the meeting?
6 Please get (a) business class ticket and ask for (a) vegetarian meal.
7 (Have you) Finished the report?
8 (I) Told (the) staff about (the) meeting.
9 (That's a) Good idea!
10 (I) Hope you've finished the report.

a The subject *I* and auxiliary verbs (*be, have, will*) can sometimes be left out.
b The subject *you* and the auxiliary can sometimes be left out of questions.
c The words *that* and *it*, and forms of the verb *be* can sometimes be left out.
d The verb *be* and a modal verb can sometimes be left out.
e The articles *the* and *a* can sometimes be left out.

Writing 1

1 Use these less formal phrases and short forms (1–10) to replace the underlined phrases (a–j) in the emails below and overleaf.

1 Can I
2 Don't forget
3 Feel free to
4 I can't make
5 I have to

6 I'm sorry to tell you
7 Can you
8 Re
9 See you tomorrow
10 Rgds

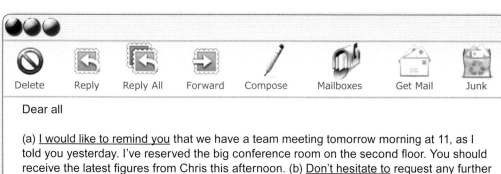

| Delete | Reply | Reply All | Forward | Compose | Mailboxes | Get Mail | Junk |

Dear all

(a) <u>I would like to remind you</u> that we have a team meeting tomorrow morning at 11, as I told you yesterday. I've reserved the big conference room on the second floor. You should receive the latest figures from Chris this afternoon. (b) <u>Don't hesitate to</u> request any further information you require.

(c) <u>I look forward to seeing you tomorrow</u>.

(d) <u>Regards</u>
Mike

Dear Mike

(e) <u>With reference to</u> your email, (f) <u>I regret to inform you</u> that (g) <u>I will not be able to attend</u> the meeting tomorrow, as (h) <u>it is necessary for me to</u> go to head office for the day.

(i) <u>I would be grateful if you could</u> give us more notice in future, and inform us about meetings several days in advance.

(j) <u>I wonder if I could</u> send Claudia to the meeting instead?

Regards
Simon

2 Which verbs in the emails above could be replaced by these less formal ones?

1 booked   2 get   3 ask for   4 need   5 tell

3 Make this email more formal by replacing the words that have been left out.

Hi Steve

Meeting went well. Pity you couldn't be there. Decided to invest up to £5m on 3 new branches in shopping centres. Will have large open counselling areas, that sort of thing, not just counters. Hope that makes you happy! Will start looking for suitable premises asap. Using agency probably quicker. Maybe TCP – think it means Town Centre Properties. Ever worked with them?

Talk to you tomorrow.

Sonia

4 The email below, written to summarize a meeting, is quite formal and long. Rewrite it using more simple language, crossing out unnecessary words and adding bullet points to make it clearer.

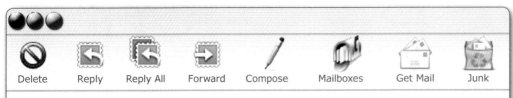

Subject: Yesterday's meeting

Dear all

This is just to summarize the key points from our meeting. Firstly, we decided to organize a survey to investigate our customers' opinions about our services. Susan will provide a brief to the marketing team and John will contact the finance department to obtain the funding so that we can commence as soon as possible.

Finally, I will ensure that the staff in the branches are informed.

Please don't hesitate to contact me if you want to discuss or verify any of these points.

Kind regards

David

Useful phrases

You will probably recognize some of the typical email phrases below, even with their words in the wrong order. Rewrite them correctly, adding capital letters and punctuation where needed.

1 if get back any problems to me there are

_____

2 week next I forward you seeing to look

_____

3 I'm report attachment sending the as an

_____

4 there's me know if anything can let do I

_____

5 form complete the asap attached please return it and

_____

6 for thanks help in advance this in matter your

_____

7 confirm call just is our to this phone

_____

8 forgot to the sorry add I attachment!

_____

Vocabulary

The words and phrases in the box are used to talk about email and web addresses. Match them to the symbols (1–10).

at	colon	dot	slash	underscore
capital (letter)	dash	lower case	small (letter)	upper case

1 .   6 _
2 :   7 ABC
3 abc   8 a
4 A   9 -
5 /   10 @

"You should check your e-mail more often. I fired you over three weeks ago."

Practice

Your department is doing some internet research on mortgages. You have to give some website addresses to a colleague, and get some addresses your colleague has. Use the **Vocabulary** above to help you.

Work in pairs. Student A should look at **page 116**, and Student B at **page 124**.

Writing 2

Look at **Practice 1** in **Unit 2**. Write an email from Kim Brown to his / her four colleagues, confirming tomorrow's meeting. Use some of the **Useful phrases** above. Use a format similar to the emails in this unit.

5 Loans and credit

AIMS

To learn about: lending decisions; key vocabulary of loans and credit
To learn how to: give advice and make suggestions
To practise: making lending decisions; giving advice to clients

Lead in

- How do commercial banks make a profit?
- How do banks decide who to lend money to?
- How do they decide what rates to lend at?
- How can large corporations raise finance?
- Why do large companies generally prefer <u>not</u> to borrow from banks?

"We'd like to lend you the money, but we're afraid we might lose you as a friend."

Reading: Banks and bonds

1 Read the texts below and then answer the questions on the opposite page.

FG Finance Glossary
www.finance-glosssary.com

Corporate bonds are issued by companies to raise capital. They are an alternative to issuing new shares on the stock market (equity finance) and are a form of debt finance. A bond is basically an IOU (short for 'I owe you') – a promise to pay back your original investment (the 'principal') at a maturity date, plus interest payments (the 'yield' or 'coupon') at regular intervals between now and then. The bond is a tradeable instrument in its own right, which means that you can buy and sell it during its life, and its value will tend to rise and fall as interest rates change.

Thirty or forty years ago, large companies that wanted to borrow money generally got loans from banks. Then they discovered that they could borrow at a lower rate by raising money directly from the public (and from institutional investors like insurance companies and pension funds), by issuing bonds. This process of disintermediation – cutting out the intermediary (the bank) between the borrower and the lenders – is obviously *not* a good thing for commercial banks. They now have to lend their money to borrowers that are less secure than large corporations.

Companies and financial institutions are given investment ratings, reflecting their financial situation and performance, by ratings companies such as Standard & Poor's and Moody's. The highest rating (AAA or Aaa) is given only to top-quality institutions, with minimal credit risk. Today, only one of these is a bank (Rabobank, in the Netherlands). The only other AAA ratings – and there are very few – belong to large corporations.

On the other hand, companies use investment banks to issue their bonds for them, permitting banks to make money from fees rather than from interest.

1 What are the two main ways in which large companies and corporations raise capital?
2 What might explain why only one bank has a AAA rating?
3 What form of income do banks now get from large companies?

2 Use a word from each box to make word combinations from the text. You can use some words more than once. Then use some of the word combinations to complete the sentences below.

credit	date
debt	finance
equity	instruments
financial	payments
interest	performance
investment	rating
maturity	risk
tradeable	situation

1 Bondholders get _____ _____ until the bond's _____
_____ .

2 Because bonds are _____ _____ you can sell them at any time, but their price will depend on the company's _____ _____ and the level of interest rates.

3 Only companies with hardly any _____ _____ get a AAA _____
_____ .

Vocabulary

You are going to listen to an interview about lending decisions. Before you listen, check your understanding of the words and phrases in the box by matching them with their definitions (1–10).

collateral	credit rating	maturity	portfolio	cost of funds
EBIT	operating cash flow	credit limit	margin	overhead costs

1 the abbreviation for a company's earnings before interest and taxes
2 all the securities and financial assets held by a financial institution or an individual
3 an evaluation of a borrower's ability to pay interest and pay back a loan in the future
4 something of value that secures a loan or other credit; if the borrower cannot repay, the lender can sell it to pay off the loan
5 the date on which a loan must be repaid, or the length of time until this date
6 the difference between the interest rate a lender pays and the rate it charges its borrowers
7 the expenses of operating a business that are not directly related to individual products or services (e.g. electricity, telephones, administrative costs)
8 the maximum amount that a bank will lend to a customer
9 the money generated from a business's normal activities
10 the price (interest rate) that a financial institution must pay for the use of money

Listening 1: Lending decisions

Gerlinde Igler works for a German bank. Listen to her talking about how banks make lending decisions for commercial and corporate customers, and complete the notes on what she says.  **5.1**

Normally the bank analyses _____

The bank has to evaluate _____

The bank discusses _____

Normally the company should be able to _____

The bank has got different limits for _____

They also have a rating for _____

Before financing foreign transactions, the bank _____

If the bank doesn't have a limit _____

Listening 2: Margins

Listen to Gerlinde Igler talking about how banks determine lending rates, and answer the questions below. **5.2**

1 What are the two factors that determine the interest rate a customer is charged?
2 What is the advantage for a business of having a Triple A or AAA rating?
3 What are the different costs involved in the calculation of the bank's margin?
4 How can a bank reduce the risks involved in granting a loan?

Advising and suggesting

1 Think of some phrases for giving advice and making suggestions or recommendations in a business situation.

Some common phrases are shown below; you will add more later.

Phrase	Example
How about *doing* ...	How about opening a savings account?
I think (that) you should *do* ...	I think you should reduce your spending.
I think (that) you ought to *do* ...	I think you ought to pay off that debt first.
It'd (It would) be a good idea *to do* ...	It'd be a good idea to pay those bills regularly.
I'd (I would) advise you (not) *to do* ...	I'd advise you to sell those stocks immediately.
It's advisable *to do* ...	It's advisable to diversify your portfolio.
Have you considered *doing* ...	Have you considered getting life assurance?

Note that a verb following *how about* and *consider* is always in the *-ing* form; a verb following *should* is always the infinitive without *to*; and a verb following *advisable* is always the infinitive with *to*.

Notice also the difference in spelling between the noun *advice* and the verb *advise*. The noun is uncountable. We do not say *an advice*; we say *some advice, a piece of advice, several pieces of advice*.

2   Which of the phrases opposite are more formal, and which more informal? Which of them would you use in a formal letter? Which would you use with a colleague you know well?

3   Can you think of any phrases using the verbs *suggest*, *recommend* and *advise*? Write them in the table opposite showing the structure that is used, and add an example for each. Use a dictionary to help if you need to.

4   Use some of the phrases opposite to give advice or make suggestions to the following people:

   1   A customer who has $5,000 in a savings account paying 2.5% p.a. and a credit card debt of $3,000 on which she is paying 1.25% per month
   2   A customer who has just had a pay rise of $1,000 a month
   3   A customer who wants to invest $50,000 in the stock of just one company
   4   A customer who has just finished paying off his mortgage and asks for a loan of $50,000 to make improvements to his house
   5   A self-employed customer without any plans for retirement
   6   A customer who wants to take €10,000 cash on a long vacation
   7   A customer who complains about the length of the queues at his local branch
   8   A shopkeeper who always keeps the day's takings at home overnight and pays them in to the bank the following morning

Practice 1

As part of a training course, a bank is asking teams of employees from different departments to give their opinion on loan applications. The bank operates at local, national and international levels. It lends to individual customers, small and medium-sized businesses, and large companies.

Your teacher will give you a role to prepare. Use the phrases for giving advice and making suggestions from the **Language focus** opposite.

Work in groups of four. Student A should look at **page 116**, Student B at **page 125**, Student C at **page 134**, and Student D at **page 132**.

Practice 2

A bank advisor is in a meeting with one of the customers from the cases in **Practice 1**. Your teacher will give you a role to prepare. Use the phrases for advising, suggesting and recommending from the **Language focus** opposite.

Work in pairs. Student A should look at **pages 117–8** and Student B at **pages 125–6**.

Writing

Following the discussion in **Practice 1**, write a brief email to the training manager, confirming the decisions made.

Dear ...
I'm writing to inform you about the decisions that were made in this morning's training exercise ...

6

Business correspondence 2

To learn about: style and standard phrases in business letters
To learn how to: reply to complaints

Lead in

- In what situations do you write a letter rather than an email?
- What kind of letters do you and your colleagues have to write at work?
- What do you find difficult about writing business letters in English?
- Does your company or institution have templates or models for standard or common letters? If so, why?

Formal and informal style 2

Business letters, sent from one company to another, or to clients and customers, are generally written in a very polite, formal style. However, it is not only letters that are written this way: the first contact between a company and a business partner is generally written in a formal style, even if it is an email. Subsequent correspondence between people who know and like each other often becomes less formal, using the style discussed in **Unit 4**. Such correspondence is increasingly done by email rather than letters (posted by 'snail-mail').

1 Which style, formal or informal, would you use for the following?

1 Writing to a customer you know well to summarize a meeting
2 Writing to someone you don't know to apply for a job
3 Writing to someone you have known for years to apply for a job
4 Complaining to a valued business partner about contractual terms that have not been respected
5 Writing to a long-time business partner with a renewed contract
6 Apologizing to a customer for bad service
7 Apologizing to a colleague for missing a meeting
8 Congratulating a member of staff for their good results

Standard phrases

Business letters often include standard sections – an opening sentence referring to previous correspondence or stating the reason for writing, a closing sentence, etc. There are fixed phrases for these, as well as for the different things you can do in a letter (give news, give information, apologize, etc.). These phrases often use longer, more formal words instead of short ones with a similar meaning (see **Unit 4**).

2 Can you think of any phrases to use for the following actions?

1 Starting a letter (referring to previous meetings or correspondence)
2 Explaining the reason for writing
3 Giving bad news
4 Giving good news
5 Giving information
6 Apologizing
7 Ending a letter

3 Now classify the following standard phrases. Which of the actions (1–7) above could they be used for?

a Do not hesitate to contact us again if you need further assistance. ☐
b Further to our meeting last Friday ... ☐
c Further to your enquiry, we are pleased to enclose ... ☐
d I regret to inform you that ... ☐
e I am just writing to confirm ... ☐
f I wish to advise you that according to the terms of our agreement ... ☐
g If you have any further questions, please contact us. ☐
h We are pleased to announce ... ☐
i We are writing to give you further information about ... ☐
j We are writing to inform you that ... ☐
k We deeply regret any inconvenience caused by ... ☐
l We look forward to hearing from you. ☐
m With reference to your enquiry of 13 May, I am enclosing details of ... ☐
n Thank you for your letter of June 14. ☐

Listening 1: A letter of complaint

Credit card fraud rising

Banks call for crackdown on credit card fraudsters

Four jailed for £3m credit card fraud

1 Listen to a telephone conversation between two colleagues at a credit card company. Which of the statements below are true? ⊘ 6.1

1 The customer's card had been used fraudulently before.
2 The customer's card had not been used fraudulently before.
3 The bank knew about the problem, but didn't do anything.
4 The bank noticed the transactions, but didn't do anything.

2 Now listen again, and answer the questions below. ⊘ 6.1

1 In what order did the following things happen?
   a The credit card company blocked the customer's credit card. ☐
   b The credit card company suspected fraudulent transactions and
      contacted the customer. ☐

c The credit card company suspected fraudulent transactions but did not contact the customer. ☐

d The customer angrily denied that the transactions were fraudulent. ☐

e The customer complained that her card had become unusable. ☐

f The customer's card reached its credit limit. ☐

g There were fraudulent transactions using the customer's card. ☐

2 Do you think the credit card company has done anything wrong?

3 Should the customer's identity make any difference to the letter the company writes?

Writing 1

1 The credit card company writes a letter to the customer in **Listening 1**. Think of a sentence that can be used in the letter to do each of the following things.

1 Express regret for the considerable inconvenience the customer has suffered.

2 Apologize for the fact that her card was being used fraudulently.

3 Explain that even though they have careful security procedures, it is impossible to completely eliminate credit card fraud.

4 Say that the card has now been blocked.

5 Reassure the customer that inquiries are underway to find out who was illegally using the card details.

6 Say that a new card and a new PIN number have been sent to her.

7 Explain that they did notice suspicious transactions, but did not immediately react because of the letter she sent them in similar circumstances last year.

8 Explain that if they had taken action (blocking the card) she would still have been in the same situation.

9 Suggest that she should not go abroad in future without an additional way of paying bills or withdrawing cash.

10 Express regret again and say they hope she will continue to use their services.

2 Now write a complete letter to the customer, explaining the situation, using the standard format shown in **Writing 3** on the next page. Remember that letters beginning *Dear Sir / Madam* usually end with *Yours faithfully*, while letters beginning *Dear + name* usually end with *Yours sincerely*. You can also use some of the **Useful phrases** below.

3 When you have finished, check your letter against other learners' letters. What are the differences? Whose version is better and why?

Useful phrases

We are very sorry to learn that ...
We greatly regret the fact that ...
At MGS Credit Cards, we do everything possible to ...
Despite all our security procedures, ...
Please be assured that we are continuing to investigate this matter fully.
This was an error on our part.
Please accept our apologies.
However, I must inform you that ...
I would also like to mention ...
For your future reference, it would be advisable to ...
We hope you will continue to ...

Listening 2: An angry phone call

Listen to an angry customer phoning a bank and answer the questions below. **6.2**

1 What has happened?   2 Whose fault is it?

Writing 2

Write a letter to Mr Hewson, the customer in **Listening 2**, using the **Useful phrases** opposite.
In the letter, you should:

- express regret for his unfortunate experience
- explain that all small business customers were informed about the closing of the night safe during renovation work
- point out that his colleagues have already used your automatic deposit machine on many occasions.

Writing 3

1 In **Listening 1** and **2**, the bank does not admit responsibility for its customer's difficulties. However, there are situations when the company needs to accept responsibility and apologize. Which of the **Useful phrases** opposite accept responsibility? Can you think of any other phrases you could use for this?

2 Read the letter below and write a reply. Apologize for the error and for the rather tactless behaviour of the bank.

Strutt Manufacturing

146 East Street, London WC3 2ET
Telephone 0207 249 3412   Fax 0207 249 3413
Email enquiries@strutt-mfg.com

Our ref: SM234   December 4, 20--

The Manager
MGS Bank
23 Ladbroke Avenue
London W11 3PX

Dear Sir

'Valued business customers'

Last week we had a meeting with you about our request for a short-term loan to cover the cost of an unpaid export order that is insured by a government export credit guarantee. For reasons which are still not clear to us, you declined to grant us the loan.

This morning I received a large envelope from you full of advertising leaflets offering me 'additional services for valued business customers'. I see that you wish to offer me a Merchant Credit Card Account (which of course we already have with another, more efficient bank), Executive Life Insurance, a TaxDirect service, a Safe Deposit Box, and various other facilities.

Unfortunately, you were not prepared to offer us the particular service that we need, and so we are clearly not one of your 'valued business customers'. We do not wish to receive further advertising material from you.

Yours faithfully

A Strutt
Managing Director

---

7 Accounting

AIMS

To learn about: types of accounting; financial statements; key vocabulary of financial statements and accounting
To learn how to: say figures in English; talk about financial statements
To practise: presenting financial results

Ahold pays $1.1bn to settle accounting scandal

Accounting scandal: Apple may have to restate profits

BP accused of 'world-class accounting scandal'

Parmalat goes bankrupt after accounting scandal

EMI shares dive after accounting scandal

WorldCom: yet another American auditing scandal

Lead in

- What is accounting? Why is it necessary for companies and organizations?
- Is there is one way of doing a business's accounts, or lots of different possible ways?
- What is auditing and why is it necessary?

Vocabulary 1

You are going to listen to Eric Sharp, a financial director, talking about accounting. Before you listen, check your understanding of the words and phrases in the box by matching them with their definitions (1–10).

assets	cost accounting	income	tax accounting	financial accounting
expenditure	liabilities	bookkeeping	management accounting	auditing

1 anything owned by a company – cash, buildings, machines, etc.
2 calculating how much tax an individual or a company should pay – or trying to reduce this figure
3 checking and evaluating financial records
4 determining the unit cost of a manufactured product, including indirect costs
5 keeping financial records and preparing financial statements
6 money that a company will have to pay to someone else – bills, debts, interest, taxes, etc.
7 recording transactions (purchases and sales) in ledgers
8 the money that a company receives from supplying goods or services
9 the money that a company spends
10 the use of a company's accounting data by its managers for planning and control

Listening 1: Types of accounting

1 Listen to Eric Sharp talking about the different branches of the accounting profession. What three roles or areas of work does he mention? **7.1**

2 Now listen again and match the two parts of the sentences below. **7.1**

1 Bookkeepers
2 Management accountants
3 Senior accountants at financial controller and director level
4 Internal auditing
5 External auditors

a is about making sure that the management has sufficient control over what is going on in the company.
b do the boring work – recording transactions in purchase ledgers and sales ledgers.
c have to verify that a company's published financial statements give a true and fair view of its profit, its assets and its liabilities.
d interpret the transactions recorded by bookkeepers.
e use accounting data to make decisions about how the business should proceed.

3 Which branches of accounting defined in **Vocabulary 1** are not mentioned by Eric Sharp? Would you be interested in working in these areas of accounting?

Listening 2: Financial statements

Listen to Eric Sharp talking about financial statements, and complete the text. **7.2**

Eric Sharp: There are three or four different statements that companies include in their Annual Reports, which (1) _____ can legally expect to see. The key documents are the profit and loss account, the balance sheet, and a funds flow statement of some kind. In the USA, and under International Financial Reporting Standards, the profit and loss account is called an income statement. This document is fairly self-explanatory: it's (2) _____ _____ _____. The balance sheet is a statement showing what the company has, and (3) _____ _____ _____ at the end of the year, while the funds flow statement attempts to show whether the company is (4) _____ _____ _____ cash. The tax authorities require more detail than is given in these documents; (5) _____ _____ is not the same as accounting profit, so they will expect to see reconciliations between the two.

Vocabulary 2

1 Investors and many people working in finance need to understand the basic terms in financial statements. Decide which of the alternatives (a–c) each definition describes.

1 A charge for arranging a transaction (e.g. buying or selling securities)
    a commission   b fee   c tax
2 A charge for a service performed by a bank
    a commission   b fee   c tax
3 Payments for an insurance policy
    a commissions   b premiums   c tariffs
4 A reduction in the value of an asset, charged against profits
    a amortization   b loss   c waste

5   Adjective meaning after all deductions have been made
    a gross   **b** net   **c** zero

6   Adjective meaning for a whole group of companies
    a consolidated   **b** corporate   **c** mutual

7   Adjective meaning one year or less in financial statements
    a annual   **b** long-term   **c** short-term

8   Part-ownership (less than 50%) of other companies
    a conglomeration   **b** liabilities   **c** minority interests

9   Things of value that cannot be physically touched, such as reputation (goodwill), brand names and trademarks
    a intangible assets   **b** liabilities   **c** tangible assets

10   The net worth of a company – the amount by which assets exceed liabilities
    a dividends   **b** profit   **c** shareholders' equity

2   **Now look at the income statement from Barclays Bank, and complete it using answers from Vocabulary 1. Some words can be used more than once.**

Barclays PLC

(1) _____ income statement – IFRS

For the year ended 31st December

	2005 £m	2004 £m
Continuing operations		
Interest income	17,232	13,880
Interest expense	(9,157)	(7,047)
Net interest income	8,075	6,833
Fee and commission income	6,430	5,509
Fee and commission expense	(725)	(662)
Net (2) _____ and (3) _____ income	5,705	4,847
Net trading income	2,321	1,487
Net investment income	858	1,027
Principal transactions	3,179	2,514
Net (4) _____ from insurance contracts	872	1,042
Other income	147	131
Total income	17,978	15,367
Net claims and benefits paid on insurance contracts	(645)	(1,259)
Total income (5) _____ of insurance claims	17,333	14,108
Impairment charge and other credit provisions	(1,571)	(1,093)
Net income	15,762	13,015
Operating expenses excluding amortisation of (6) _____ (7) _____	(10,448)	(8,514)
Amortisation of (8) _____ (9) _____	(79)	(22)
Operating expenses	(10,527)	(8,536)
Share of post-tax results of associates and joint ventures	45	56
Profit on disposal of associates and joint ventures	–	45
Profit before tax	5,280	4,580
(10) _____	(1,439)	(1,279)
Net profit for the year	3,841	3,301

IFRS = International Financial Reporting Standards

Talking about figures 1

In British English, *and* is used after *hundred* when saying figures; in American English it is not.

Example: 1,234,567,890

(British English) *one billion, two hundred and thirty-four million, five hundred and sixty-seven thousand, eight hundred and ninety*

(American English) *one billion, two hundred thirty-four million, five hundred sixty-seven thousand, eight hundred ninety*

Barclays' consolidated statements are expressed in millions of pounds sterling; to get the total figure you need to add six zeros. For example, their operating expenses were £10,527,000,000: ten billion, five hundred (and) twenty-seven million pounds. These large figures can also be said as decimals: ten point five two seven billion pounds. See **Unit 9** for more on saying decimal numbers.

1   Work in pairs and take turns to test your partner. One person finds one of the following figures from the income statement, and reads it out. The other person says which figure (1–6) it is. Use a calculator if you need to.

    1   the largest figure
    2   the largest negative figure (in brackets)
    3   total income over the two years
    4   total net profit over the two years
    5   total tax paid over the two years
    6   the increase in operating expenses since the previous year

2   Work in pairs. Ask your partner how much time, in hours or minutes, they think they spend in an average week doing the following things:

    1   working
    2   working in English
    3   using a computer
    4   eating
    5   sleeping
    6   watching television
    7   waiting at red traffic lights.

    Calculate how many seconds they spend on each activity per year. Read out the figures while your partner writes them down, and then check that you both have the same figures.

Listening 3: Barclays' balance sheet

Look at the balance sheet on **page 40**, and then listen to a journalist talking about the bank. Make notes on what the journalist says, and fill in the five missing figures. **🔘 7.3**

Barclays PLC

Consolidated balance sheet summary – IFRS
As at 31st December

	2005 £m	2004 £m
Assets		
Cash and other short-term funds	5,807	3,525
Treasury bills and other eligible bills	n/a	6,658
Trading and financial assets designated at fair value	251,820	n/a
Derivative financial instruments	136,823	n/a
Debt securities and equity shares	n/a	141,710
Loans and advances to banks	31,105	80,632
Loans and advances to customers	(1) _____	262,409
Available for sale investments	53,497	n/a
Reverse repurchase agreements and cash collateral on securities borrowed	160,398	n/a
Insurance assets, including unit-linked assets	114	8,576
Property, plant and equipment	(2) _____	2,282
Other assets	13,143	32,389
Total assets	(3) _____	538,181
Liabilities		
Deposits and items in the course of collection due to banks	77,468	112,229
Customer accounts	(4) _____	217,492
Trading and financial liabilities designated at fair value	104,949	n/a
Liabilities to customers under investment contracts	85,201	n/a
Derivative financial instruments	137,971	n/a
Debt securities in issue	103,328	83,842
Repurchase agreements and cash collateral on securities lent	121,178	n/a
Insurance contract liabilities, including unit-linked liabilities	3,767	8,377
Subordinated liabilities	12,463	12,277
Other liabilities	14,918	87,200
Total liabilities	899,927	521,417
Shareholders' equity		
Shareholders' equity excluding minority interests	17,426	15,870
Minority interests	7,004	894
Total shareholders' equity	(5) _____	16,764
Total liabilities and shareholders' equity	924,357	538,181

n/a = 'not applicable'
IFRS = International Financial Reporting Standards

Practice

You are the Chief Financial Officer at Barclays, presenting the 2005 results to the Board of Directors. Give the most important figures, such as:
- the income received from interest, fees and commissions, trading, and insurance premiums
- the net income
- the pre-tax and after-tax profit
- the value of the group's assets, liabilities, and shareholders' equity.

You can also report how much higher or lower these figures are compared to the previous year, the annual percentage increase or decrease, and some reasons for the changes. Use a calculator if you need to.

8 Socializing

Lead in

- How often do you need to use English with visitors at work, or how often will you need to in the future?
- What do you find difficult about making 'small talk' in English?

Listening 1: Greeting people and making introductions

1 Listen to Monica Steiner, who works for a Swiss multinational company, being met by two American colleagues at an airport in New York, and answer the questions below. **◎ 8.1**

   1 Has Monica met her colleagues before? How do you know?
   2 What questions do they ask Monica?

2 In the dialogue, Monica, Michael and Siobhan use typical phrases for greetings and introductions. Listen again and write their responses in the table below. You will add more phrases later. **◎ 8.1**

Greeting or question	Response
Hi. I'm ...	
Do you know ...?	
How are you?	

3 Monica's response 'How do you do?' can also be used as a greeting. What is the response? What is the difference between this greeting and Siobhan's 'How are you?'

4 Now add any other phrases you know for greetings, introductions and their responses to the table on **page 41**.

Discussion

- In your country, do people generally want to talk socially to new or potential business partners, to get to know a bit about them, before starting a business meeting or negotiation? Why is (or isn't) this considered important?
- Which countries and cultures do you think find social relations very important in business? Put the following countries in order. Which of them do you think spend the most time in small talk or socializing before a meeting, or before agreeing to do business?

| Brazil | China | Germany | Russia |
| Britain | Egypt | Japan | USA |

- In **Listening 1**, Michael and Siobhan make small talk, asking Monica some social questions after welcoming her. Make a short list of topics you could talk about before getting down to business in the following situations, and think of one or two questions you could ask for each topic.

1 As soon as you meet someone (at an airport or at reception in your company)
2 Later, over a drink or a meal

Making small talk and keeping the conversation going

1 Here is part of a typical small talk dialogue between a visitor and a colleague in a company in Dubai. Write the questions (1–5).

1 _____?
Oh no, I've been here quite often.

2 _____?
Late on Tuesday evening. The flight was delayed, unfortunately.

3 _____?
Only until Friday – I want to get home for the weekend.

4 _____?
At the Hyatt. It's a very nice hotel.

5 _____?
Well, I was born in London, but I live in Brighton now.

2 When you are making small talk, you can keep the conversation going by asking more 'open' questions, or by adding a question to the end of your replies. The two colleagues above continue their conversation. Underline the phrases the visitor, Andrew, uses to keep the conversation going.

Andrew: Do you live in the city?

Rachid: No I live in Ajman.

Andrew: I haven't been there. What's it like?

Rachid: It's smaller than here, with old buildings and modern ones too, and a port.

Andrew: I like old buildings. And do you have a family?

Rachid: Yes, I've got two children: a girl and a boy. They're 17 and 14.

Andrew: I've got two boys; they're 12 and 9. And what do you do in your spare time?

Rachid: I love skydiving.

Andrew: Really? I've never tried that. Isn't it dangerous?

Rachid: No, it's fun – and you always have a parachute! So, are you doing anything later? Would you like to join me for dinner?

Andrew: I'm afraid I can't make it tonight; I have another engagement. How about tomorrow?

Rachid: Yes, why don't we leave early, and I can drive you to Ajman – I know a good seafood restaurant there.

Andrew: Thank you. That sounds great.

3 What phrases does Andrew use to do the following?

1 Decline an invitation
2 Accept an invitation

Some general 'rules' for doing business in a foreign language:
Use relatively formal language at first. When you become familiar with the normal style of the people you're dealing with, you can try to copy it (and become less formal if they are).

Don't try to use <u>very</u> informal or colloquial language yourself, unless you know that you are good at it.

Be polite. Begin questions and requests with polite phrases.

Examples: *Excuse me ...*
I'm sorry, ...
Please would you ...?
Would you mind ...?

If you don't understand or hear something, say so immediately.

Examples: *I'm sorry, I didn't hear / catch / understand that.*
Sorry, could you repeat that, please?

Practice 1

You are going to practise social language in two situations: greeting a visitor at the reception desk, and making small talk after a meeting. Your teacher will give you a role to prepare. Use the language for greetings, introductions and small talk from **Listening 1** and the **Language focus**.

Work in pairs. Student A should look at **page 118**, and Student B at **page 127**.

Discussion

- Some cultures have very strong 'rules' of protocol or etiquette – what behaviour is acceptable, which procedures are correct, etc.

  In your country, do you have formal rituals, such as bowing, or exchanging business cards, which show individuals' status and other people's acceptance of this status?

- Do you use first names, family names, or job titles ('Mr President') in meetings and negotiations?

- If your country doesn't do these things, do you know any countries that do?

Listening 2: Talking about your career

Listen to Michael and Monica discussing their careers over a cup of coffee, and complete the tapescript below. 🔊 **8.2**

Michael: How long have you worked in the finance department at Head Office?

Monica: Two years. I (1) _____ _____ a job there in my last year at university, when I was studying finance and economics, but I didn't even (2) _____ _____ _____. So I went to London and worked as a (3) _____ in a British bank for six months. After that joined a Swiss bank where I worked in the corporate department. Then I was (4) _____ to their trade finance department. But I didn't get (5) _____ so after three years I applied to this company again, and they offered me my present job. I really like what I'm doing now. I find financial planning really interesting. I'm (6) _____ _____ some very big projects. What about you?

Michael: Well, I studied (7) _____ at university and then worked for an (8) _____ _____ for two years, but I didn't like it. So I did an MBA, and then got a job here. Now, as you know, I'm in production and operations. I'm (9) _____ _____ _____ setting up new production facilities here, which is why I'm working on this project with you, and I'm also (10) _____ _____ two projects in Canada. Which means I'm always (11) _____ _____ lots of problems at the same time. But I enjoy the (12) _____!

Useful phrases

Phrases you can use when talking about your career include:

I studied ...
When I left college / university I applied for ...
I joined ...
I left after ... years ... because I wanted to ...
I got a job with ...
I was transferred to ...
Now I'm responsible for ... and I have to deal with ...
The job involves ...
I was promoted to ...
I expect to be promoted to ...
In the future I want to ...

Practice 2

Give a summary of your career so far. Imagine you are speaking to a new business partner. If you have not yet started working, imagine a career you would like, and give a summary of that. Use the **Useful phrases** above.

Listening 3: Saying goodbye

Monica Steiner is saying goodbye to Michael in New York before flying back to Switzerland. What phrases do they use to do these things? **8.3**

1 Say it's time to leave

_____

2 Say positive things about their meeting (2 phrases)

_____

_____

3 Mention a future contact (2 phrases)

_____

_____

4 Offer a phone number

_____

5 Confirm transport to the airport

_____

Practice 3

You are going to practise social language at the end of a meeting. Your teacher will give you a role to prepare. Use the language for saying goodbye from **Listening 3**.

Work in pairs. Student A should look at **page 118**, and Student B at **page 127**.

9 Central banking

AIMS

To learn about: the functions of central banks; monetary policy; key
  vocabulary of central banking and monetary policy
To learn how to: say decimal numbers
To practise: talking about central banking decisions and policies

Lead in

- What are the functions of a central bank?
- How can the actions of a central bank affect individuals as well as companies?

Discussion

Which of the following would you expect a central bank to do? Mark them A = always,
S = sometimes, or N = never.

1   act as banker to the government and the commercial banks
2   attempt to influence the exchange rate
3   clear cheques between commercial banks
4   decide the country's minimum interest rate
5   decide all of a country's interest rates
6   issue banknotes
7   issue securities for companies
8   issue securities for the government
9   keep minimum deposits of commercial banks' reserves
10 lend money to banks in difficulty
11 lend money to small businesses
12 maintain financial stability
13 manage reserves of gold and foreign currencies
14 manage the assets of wealthy individuals
15 publish monetary and banking statistics
16 supervise the banking system

Vocabulary

You are going to read about the major functions of the Bank of England. Before you read, check
your understanding of the words (1–9) below by matching them with their definitions (a–i).

1	policy	a	a level or situation which you intend to achieve
2	threats	b	a general, continuous increase in prices
3	oversight	c	an agreed plan of what to do
4	target	d	basic and most important
5	core (adjective)	e	in good condition
6	sound (adjective)	f	paid
7	sterling	g	potential sources of danger
8	inflation	h	supervision
9	remunerated	i	the name of the British currency

Reading: The Bank of England

1 A student has made notes during a lecture about the role of the Bank of England. Read them quickly and decide which of the functions listed in the **Discussion** activity opposite are included in the Bank of England's work, and which are not mentioned.

The Bank of England has two (1) _____ purposes. One is ensuring monetary stability, i.e. having stable prices – low (2) _____ – and consequently confidence in the currency.

The government sets an inflation (3) _____, and the Bank's Monetary Policy Committee tries to meet it by raising or lowering the official interest rate when necessary.

UK banks and building societies have to hold reserves at the Bank. These are (4) _____ at the Bank's official interest rate. If British banks need to borrow short-term funds they do this in the (5) _____ money markets.

The Bank can influence the amount of money and the interest rates in these markets – this is how it implements its monetary (6) _____.

The Bank also deals in the foreign exchange market. It can use the UK's foreign currency and gold reserves to try to influence the exchange rate if needed.

The Bank's other core purpose is to maintain the stability of the financial system. The Bank has to detect and reduce any (7) _____ to financial stability, and make sure the overall system is safe and secure. It monitors and analyses the behaviour of the major participants in the financial system and the wider financial and economic environment, and tries to identify potential risks. A (8) _____ and stable financial system is important, and is also necessary for carrying out monetary policy efficiently.

The Bank's role also includes (9) _____ of payment systems for transactions between individuals, businesses and financial institutions.

The Bank sometimes acts as 'lender of last resort' to financial institutions in difficulty, to prevent panic or a loss of confidence spreading through the whole financial system.

2 Complete the text with the words (1–9) from the **Vocabulary** exercise opposite.

3 According to the text, are the following statements true or false?

1 The Bank of England wants to prevent prices rising.
2 The government sets a figure for what it thinks should be the maximum inflation rate.
3 The government makes decisions about interest rates.
4 Commercial banks have to keep some of their funds at the Bank of England.
5 The Bank does not pay interest on commercial banks' deposits.
6 The Bank can try to change the sterling exchange rate.
7 The Bank has to eliminate threats to financial stability.
8 The Bank supervises the clearing system: the settlement of claims between banks.
9 The Bank always lends money to financial institutions in danger of going bankrupt.

4 Use a word or phrase from each box to make word combinations from the text. You can use some words more than once. Then use the correct form of some of the word combinations to complete the sentences below.

identify	exchange rates
implement	policies
influence	risks
maintain	stability
reduce	threats

1 Just like the central bank, all companies have to try to _____ potential financial _____.

2 The Bank can spend the country's currency reserves in order to _____ _____ _____.

3 The Bank can try to _____ _____ to the financial system, but it can't eliminate them completely.

4 The Bank has to _____ the _____ of the financial system, but that doesn't mean it rescues irresponsible banks.

5 The Bank _____ _____ that should enable it to meet the inflation target set by the government.

Listening 1: Monetary policy

1 You are going to listen to Kate Barker, an economist and a member of the Bank of England's Monetary Policy Committee, talking about monetary policy. Before you listen, try to answer the questions below.

1 What is the aim of monetary policy?
2 What tools does a central bank use to control supply and demand for money?
3 What tends to happen when interest rates rise?
4 What tends to happen when interest rates fall?
5 What do commercial banks do after the central bank changes the base rate at which it lends them money?

2 Now listen to Kate Barker, and compare your answers with what she says. 🎧 **9.1**

3 Check your understanding of the language Kate Barker uses by matching the words in the box with their definitions (1–8).

base rate	consume	incentive	plant
capital	demand	labour	supply

1 encouragement or a reason to do something
2 factories, and the machines and equipment in them
3 money invested in companies, to buy buildings, machinery, etc.
4 the quantity of goods and services offered for sale by companies
5 the rate at which the central bank lends money to commercial banks
6 to spend money on goods and services
7 what people consume and how much they invest
8 work done by people employed by businesses

Discussion

Go back to the first **Discussion** exercise. According to what you have learnt from the **Reading** and **Listening** exercises, which of the 16 activities listed are done by central banks?

Talking about figures 2

When discussing interest rates and monetary policy, you need to know how to say decimal numbers.

English uses a symbol like a full stop between the two parts of a decimal number. It is called a *decimal point*. A comma is not used in this position. In a pure number (without a unit of measurement), each digit after the decimal point is said separately.

Examples:

3.5	*three point five*
3.51	*three point five one* (<u>not</u> *three point fifty-one*)
3.14159	*three point one four one five nine*
3.75%	*three point seven five percent*

However, if the number after a decimal represents a unit of money, length, etc., it is usually read as a normal number.

Examples:

$5.61	*five dollars sixty-one* (*cents*)
1.22 m	*one metre twenty-two* (*centimetres*)

0 is called *zero* or (mainly in British English) *nought*. British English also uses *oh*, but only <u>after</u> the decimal point, never before.

Examples:

11.005	*eleven point oh oh five* (or *eleven point double oh five*)
0.501	*zero / nought point five oh one*
0.001	*zero / nought point oh oh one* (or *zero / nought point double oh one*)

Read the following sentences out loud:

1 Right now, the euro's worth $1.0829.
2 That's up 0.00094 from yesterday.
3 The Bank of England's base rate is 3.75%.
4 0.001 is also called ten to the power minus 3.
5 The share's trading at $5.41.

Listening 2: Saying figures

Listen to the ten sentences on the recording, and write down the figures you hear.

Practice

Decide what you think a central bank would typically do in the following situations, and then explain why to the class. Use some of the new vocabulary from this unit.

1 A provincial savings bank has bad debts of $300 million and may go bankrupt because it lent too much money to property speculators, and the value of their investments has gone down by 40%.
2 Inflation has increased by 1.25% in three months, which is half the country's annual inflation target. The economy seems to be working at full capacity.
3 A trader at a large universal bank has lost $450 million in disastrous derivatives trades. This bank now has absolutely no liquidity.
4 Demand for consumer goods has declined for the sixth successive month, and unemployment has increased by 1.75% in three months.

10 Meetings 1

To learn how to: chair a meeting; deal with interruptions and digressions
To learn about: key vocabulary of meetings

Lead in

- Are business meetings always necessary? Are they ever enjoyable?
- What kind of meetings do you think are most worthwhile?
- What kind of meetings do you think are least worthwhile?
- Are meetings sometimes too long? How much time do you spend in meetings, and how could this be reduced?

Discussion

Meetings are not the same all over the world. Answer the following questions for your company, or your country or part of the world.

- Is punctuality important? Do meetings have to begin exactly on time?
- Is it important to reach an agreement quickly ('time is money'), or are getting to know people and reaching a consensus more important than speed?
- Who has the power to make decisions – an individual (usually the most senior person at the meeting), or a group?
- Is it acceptable to show your emotions in a meeting or negotiation?
- Can you suggest parts of the world where people generally do these things differently from in your country?
- Do you think that corporate culture – a company's ways of operating and its values, beliefs and principles – is more important than the nationality of the participants or the location of the meeting?

Vocabulary

Check your understanding of words and phrases for organizing and controlling meetings (1–6) by matching them with their definitions (a–f).

1 any other business (AOB)
2 apologies for absence
3 compromise
4 consensus
5 to digress
6 minutes

a to move off the subject and start talking about something else
b a written report distributed to participants after a meeting
c often the last item in a meeting, when participants discuss issues not on the agenda
d a way of reaching agreement in which each side concedes or gives up something it wants
e the situation in which most or all of the people at a meeting agree about something
f often the first item in a meeting, concerning people who cannot be present

Listening 1: Chairing a meeting

1   You are going to listen to a meeting at the head office of the National Union Bank in London.
    Before you listen, think of phrases that the person chairing a meeting could use to do the following things.

1 Welcome people to a meeting:	
2 Begin a meeting:	
3 Explain the meeting's objectives:	
4 Introduce the agenda:	
5 Explain that someone can't come:	
6 Invite someone to speak:	
7 Interrupt a speaker:	
8 Stop someone interrupting a speaker:	
9 Stop someone digressing:	
10 Thank a speaker for a contribution:	
11 Summarize what has been said:	
12 Move on to another item:	

2 Now listen to part of the meeting at the National Union Bank, and answer the questions below. *◎10.1*

    1 What is the purpose of the meeting?

    2 Which of the following things does the person chairing the meeting do?

        a Change the agenda
        b Introduce the first speaker
        c Refer to the agenda
        d Ask for participants' opinions
        e Refer to the previous meeting
        f Set the date of the next meeting
        g Give his own opinion
        h Report apologies for absence
        i State the objective of the meeting
        j Thank people for coming

3 What phrases does the chair use for functions 1, 3 and 6 in the table on page 51? Add them to the table.

Listening 2: Interruptions and digressions

Listen to another part of the meeting at the National Union Bank, and answer the questions below. *◎10.2*

    1 Which of the functions (1–12) in the table on **page 51** does the chair do in this part of the meeting?

    2 What phrases does the chair use for functions 8, 9 and 11 in the table in **Listening 1**? Add them to the table.

    3 Are the following statements true or false?

        1 The meeting is about whether it is right or wrong to move the bank's telephone operations to India.

        2 The meeting is about costs that would be involved in moving the bank's telephone operations to India.

        3 The Indian staff would require language training.

        4 Susan is worried about the expenses involved in dismissing the British call centre staff.

        5 Alice thinks the two Indian companies are asking for too much money.

        6 Susan doesn't think the bank's customers will like having a subcontractor's staff answering their telephone enquiries.

Discussion

In the meeting you have just heard, Susan feels free to interrupt Alice, as she feels very strongly about the subject. The chair politely intervenes to stop her interruption and keep the meeting on track. Could you interrupt like this in your culture? What would happen if you did?

Controlling meetings

1 Here are some other phrases used for controlling meetings. Look at the table in **Listening 1** and match these phrases to the table categories (1–12). The first one has been done as an example. There is more than one phrase for some categories.

a As you can see from the agenda, there are three points ...   4
b I think we should move on to the next topic on the agenda.   ___
c I'd like to ask Lisa to tell us about ...   ___
d It's ten o'clock. Let's start.   ___
e Just a moment. Please, let Lisa finish.   ___
f OK, I'd like to sum up the main points so far.   ___
g One at a time, please. Can we let John finish?   ___
h So, let me summarize that. You mean ...   ___
i Sorry, we can't consider that question at the moment.   ___
j Thank you Frank, I think you've made your point now.   ___
k Thank you very much Lisa, for explaining the background.   ___
l That's not what we're here to talk about. Can we stick to the agenda, please?   ___
m We're here today to talk about ... and to decide ...   ___
n Welcome, everybody. Thank you for coming.   ___

2 Now write the phrases in the table in **Listening 1**.

Practice

MGS Bank has a traineeship scheme which takes on six foreign students for two months every summer. They work on projects, and get two hours of training each week. The training department is having a meeting to discuss various inexpensive options to improve the trainees' knowledge of finance and English.

Your teacher will give you a role to prepare. Use the language for chairing and controlling meetings from this unit.

Work in groups of four. Student A should look at **page 118**, Student B at **page 127**, Student C at **page 135**, and Student D at **page 132**.

"Well, someone must have wanted this meeting."

11 Financing international trade

AIMS

To learn about: letters of credit and bills of exchange; key vocabulary of
letters of credit and bills of exchange
To learn how to: check and confirm information
To practise: checking and confirming information about financial products

Lead in

- What are your country's main exports?
- What are your country's main imports?
- Which countries or regions are your country's major trading partners?
- What are the most common ways for importers to pay exporters for goods?

Vocabulary

You are going to read about a common way of financing foreign trade. Before you read, check
your understanding of the terms in the box by using them to label the two definitions below.

> Bill of exchange   Letter of credit

Finance

The Encyclopedia

(1) _____

A method of payment for goods in which the buyer's bank guarantees to
pay a specified amount of money to the seller on presentation of specific
documents, before a certain date and according to the International Chamber
of Commerce rules.

(2) _____

An order written by an exporter instructing an importer to pay a specified
amount of money at a specified time.

Reading: How a letter of credit works

1   Read about the first four steps in a transaction involving a letter of credit, and number the
    steps 1 to 4, using the diagram opposite to help you.

☐ The advising bank authenticates the letter of credit and sends the beneficiary (the
seller) the details. The seller examines the details of the letter of credit to make sure
that he or she can meet all the conditions. If necessary, he or she contacts the buyer
and asks for amendments to be made.

☐ The applicant (the buyer) completes a contract with the seller.

☐ The issuing bank (the buyer's bank) approves the application and sends the letter of credit details to the seller's bank (the advising bank).

☐ The buyer fills in a letter of credit application form and sends it to his or her bank for approval.

❶ CONTRACT

Advice of **❹** Seller   Buyer **❷** Letter of
letter of credit   credit application

❸ L / C

Advising /
Confirming bank   Issuing bank

2 Now read about the next six steps, and number them 5 to 10 using the diagram below.

☐ If the documents are in order, the advising bank sends them to the issuing bank for payment or acceptance. If the details are not correct, the advising bank tells the seller and waits for corrected documents or further instructions.

☐ The advising/confirming bank pays the seller and notifies him or her that the payment has been made.

☐ The issuing bank advises the advising (or confirming) bank that the payment has been made.

☐ The issuing bank (the buyer's bank) examines the documents from the advising bank. If they are in order, the bank releases the documents to the buyer, pays the money promised or agrees to pay it in the future, and advises the buyer about the payment. (If the details are not correct, the issuing bank contacts the buyer for authorization to pay or accept the documents.) The buyer collects the goods.

☐ The seller presents the documents to his or her bankers (the advising bank). The advising bank examines these documents against the details on the letter of credit and the International Chamber of Commerce rules.

☐ When the seller (beneficiary) is satisfied with the conditions of the letter of credit, he or she ships the goods.

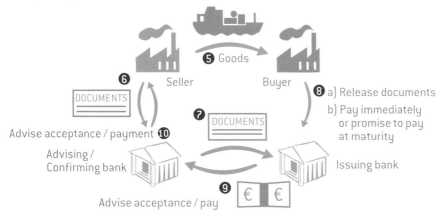

❺ Goods

❻ Seller   Buyer

DOCUMENTS

❽ a) Release documents
b) Pay immediately
or promise to pay
at maturity

❼ DOCUMENTS

Advise acceptance / payment **❿**

Advising /
Confirming bank   Issuing bank

❾ € €

Advise acceptance / pay

Listening: Asking for information about bills of exchange

1 An inexperienced exporter calls his bank's trade finance department, to get more information about bills of exchange. Listen to the conversation, and answer the questions below. *11*

    1 In a standard bill of exchange, who are the drawer, the drawee and the payee?

    2 What is the difference between a bank draft and a trade draft?

    3 Why doesn't the seller of goods have to wait until the bill or draft matures before getting paid?

    4 Why isn't an endorsed bill paid at 100%?

2 The caller uses several expressions that are commonly used to ask for repetition and clarification when you don't understand something. What are they?

Checking and confirming information

1 Look at the phrases that were used for checking and confirming information in the **Listening** exercise. Can you add any other phrases you could use in the following situations?

    1 You didn't hear what somebody has said

    2 You don't understand what somebody has said

    3 You don't think somebody is being clear or precise enough

Asking for repetition

If you didn't hear what somebody has said, you can use the following phrases. The questions have a rising intonation at the end.

> *Sorry?*
> *Pardon?*
> *Excuse me?*
> *I didn't quite catch that.*
> *I didn't hear what you said.*
> *Could you repeat that, please?*
> *Would you mind repeating that, please?*
> *I didn't quite catch what you said.*
> *I missed the first / last part.*
> *Could you say that again, please?*

If you don't understand what somebody has said, you can use some of the phrases in the **Listening** exercise, or you can say:

> *I don't understand what you've said.*
> *Could you explain that again, please?*
> *Could you rephrase that?*

Asking for clarification

If you think somebody isn't being clear or precise enough, you can say:

> *What exactly do you mean by ...?*
> *Could we have some more details, please?*
> *Could you go into more detail about ...?*
> *Can you be more specific?*
> *Could you elaborate on that a little?*
> *Do you have any examples?*
> *Can you say a little bit more about ..., please?*

Asking for verification

If you want to check that you have understood what somebody has said, you can repeat the end of their sentence with a rising intonation, and a stress on the important word:

> *The flight is <u>cancelled</u>?*

Or ask a question, with a rising intonation, and a stress on the important word:

> *Did you say '<u>cancelled</u>'?*

If someone is asking you questions to verify information, you can reply with phrases like these, to reassure them, or to clarify or rephrase something:

> *Yes, that's right.*
> *Yes, that's exactly what it means.*
> *No, it's not cancelled, only delayed.*
> *No, 'put back' means delayed. Your flight will now depart at midnight.*
> *I'm sorry, let me rephrase that.*
> *Let me explain that again.*

2 Now decide how you would reply to the following:

1 I think we need to _____ the budget by 10%.	**2** We need to send the beneficiary the details.	**3** I'm afraid we can't meet all of these conditions.
(You don't hear one of the words.)	(You don't understand the word *beneficiary*.)	(You need more information about which conditions.)

Practice

A customer calls a bank asking for clarification of some terms on the bank's web page used in import and export contracts. The call centre employee tries to answer the customer's questions. The bank's web page is shown on the next page.

Incoterms determine who pays for all the costs of international trade: transportation (or carriage), loading and unloading goods, insurance, customs duties, etc. The different terms, usually abbreviated to three-letter codes, are used all over the world, and so avoid uncertainties about whether the buyer or the seller is responsible for paying for something.

Your teacher will give you a role to prepare. In the phone call, use phrases for checking and confirming from the **Language focus** above.

Work in pairs. Student A should look at **page 118**, and Student B at **page 127**.

MGS **|||** Incoterms

Home

Application
Forms

Bill of Exchange

Contact us

FAQ's

Fee Schedule

Glossary

Incoterms

Products &
Services

Publications
and Links

Site Map

Trade Insurance

Privacy
Statement

Terms and
Conditions

Introducing Incoterms

Incoterms – short for 'International Commercial Terms' – are standard trade definitions devised and published by the International Chamber of Commerce (ICC). They are an internationally recognized code that simplifies trade between different countries.

Incoterms identify the additional costs, over and above the cost of the goods, that the seller will invoice the buyer in international sales contracts. They define who is responsible for arranging and paying for transportation, documentation, customs clearance and transport insurance.

There are 13 different Incoterms, grouped into 4 different categories.

Group 1 – The E Term (Departure)
EXW – Ex Works (named place)
Under this shipping term the seller makes the goods available for collection by the buyer at the seller's own premises. The buyer arranges insurance against damage to the goods in transit.
This term involves the least risk for, and requires the least effort by, the seller, but should not be used where the buyer cannot carry out export formalities.

Group 2 – The F Terms (Free, main carriage not paid by the seller)
FCA – Free Carrier (named place)
FAS – Free Alongside Ship (named port of shipment)
FOB – Free On Board (named port of shipment)
The seller arranges and pays for the pre-carriage in the country of export. The goods are delivered to a carrier appointed by the buyer. The buyer arranges insurance against damage to the goods in transit.

Group 3 – The C Terms (Main carriage paid by the seller)
CFR – Cost and Freight (named port of destination)
CIF – Cost, Insurance and Freight (named port of destination)
CPT – Carriage Paid To (named place of destination)
CIP – Carriage and Insurance Paid To (named place of destination)
In this group the seller arranges and pays for the main contract of carriage.
In the terms CIF and CIP the seller arranges insurance against damage to the goods in transit.

Group 4 – The D Terms (Delivered/Arrival)
DAF – Delivered At Frontier (named place)
DES – Delivered Ex Ship (named port of destination)
DEQ – Delivered Ex Quay (named port of destination)
DDU – Delivered Duty Unpaid (named place of destination)
DDP – Delivered Duty Paid (named place of destination)
These terms maximize the seller's cost and risk, as he has to make the goods available at the agreed destination. The seller bears the costs and risks of bringing the goods to the country of destination, and arranges and pays for insurance against damage to the goods in transit.

12 Meetings 2

To learn how to: conclude a meeting; ask for and give opinions; agree and disagree

To practise: holding a meeting about a call centre

Lead in

Read the quiz below, and then discuss the answers in pairs or groups.

Meetings quiz

1 When should you call a meeting?
   a Every time your group needs to share information.
   b When a meeting is the best way to achieve your objective.
   c Never, because meetings are nearly always a waste of time.

2 Who should participate?
   a People who are good at telling jokes and making meetings fun.
   b The people who can help fulfil the meeting's objective.
   c The whole department, because you don't want to exclude anyone.

3 How can you stop a meeting from going on too long?
   a You set a time limit in advance and you stick to it.
   b You can't; I don't remember the last meeting I went to that didn't run over time.
   c You have the meeting in a room without chairs and make everybody stand – that way they talk a lot less.

4 At the end of the meeting, what should the leader do?
   a Set a time and place to continue with the rest of the agenda.
   b Summarize, and remind all the participants of who is now responsible for what, and by when.
   c Offer to buy everybody a drink.

Vocabulary

1 Cross out the verb in each list that does <u>not</u> make a word combination with the noun on the right. The first one has been done as an example.

1   approve / circulate / draw up / go through / ~~hold~~ / put something on   an agenda
2   arrive at / break / carry out / implement / reach / take   a decision
3   call / call off / chair / close / hold / take   a meeting
4   approve / distribute / go through / set / take / write   the minutes
5   achieve / agree on / deal with / move towards / reach / set   an objective
6   agree with / ask for / express / find / give / hold   an opinion
7   approve / carry out / do / implement / present / reject   a plan
8   avoid / deal with / get round / overcome / put / tackle   a problem
9   agree on / arrive at / look after / come up with / find / offer   a solution
10 agree with / come to / consider / dismiss / put forward / reject   a suggestion

2 Complete the sentences using the correct form of verbs from the **Vocabulary** exercise.

1 At the beginning of every meeting, we _____ the agenda, and then we appoint someone to _____ the minutes so we have a record of what happened.
2 That was the first time I've had to _____ a meeting, and I found controlling everybody rather difficult.
3 It's better to _____ the agenda a couple of days before a meeting, so that people can prepare themselves.
4 It's very easy to _____ an objective; it's more difficult to _____ it.
5 We _____ a regular meeting every Monday morning where we try to _____ any problems that have come up.
6 I was very disappointed because the Board totally _____ my plan.
7 They argued for an hour, until someone _____ a new suggestion.

Asking for and giving opinions, agreeing and disagreeing

1 Look at the following phrases for giving strong opinions. Can you add any phrases for giving neutral or weak opinions?

I'm (absolutely) sure / convinced / positive that ...
I have absolutely no doubt that ...
I strongly believe that ...
I definitely think that ...
I really do think that ...
It's obvious that ...
Clearly / Obviously ...

2 The following phrases are used to ask for opinions. Which of them show that the speaker has a different opinion?

Do you really think / believe that ...?
What's your view on ...?
Do you think / believe / consider that ...?
Don't you think that ...?
What do you think about ...?
I'd like to hear what you think about ...
Are you absolutely sure / convinced / positive that ...?

3 The phrases below are used for weak or tentative agreement. Can you add any phrases for strong agreement?

You may / might / could be right, but ... *I agree with you, but ...*
I agree up to a point. *I agree to a certain extent.*

4 Mark the phrases for disagreeing – S if they disagree strongly, and W if the disagreement is weak or neutral.

Really? Do you think so? *I completely disagree with that.*
I'm afraid I don't agree. *I'm afraid I can't agree with that.*
Nonsense! / Rubbish! *I'm against that, because ...*
I'm not totally convinced, because ... *I can't support that, because ...*
I totally disagree with you. *I don't agree.*

Practice 1

You are going to practise expressing your opinions, asking your partner's opinions, and agreeing or disagreeing with them. Use the phrases for expressing opinions, agreeing and disagreeing from the **Language focus**.

Work in pairs. Student A should look at **page 119**, and Student B at **page 128**.

Listening: Concluding a meeting

1 You are going to listen to the end of a meeting. Before you listen, think about what the chair needs to do. What language can be used?

2 In Unit 3, you had a meeting to decide whether the MGS Bank should upgrade and modernize its branches, or try to get its customers to use the telephone and the internet. The bank has chosen to refurbish some of its branches (to redesign and renovate them) and to relocate others. Listen to the end of a meeting involving the senior managers. What phrases does the chair use to do the things listed below? **⊘12**

1 End discussion of a point
2 Begin to summarize the decisions that have been taken
3 Make sure that everyone has understood
4 Arrange the next meeting
5 Thank everybody

3 Now match the following phrases (a–g) to the functions (1–5) in the exercise above.

a Can we leave this point now and move on to the next item? ☐
b Is January 11 convenient as a date for our next meeting? ☐
c I'd like to sum up the main points. ☐
d OK. So we have decided that ... ☐
e Thank you all for coming; I think we've made a lot of progress. ☐
f Is everyone OK with that? ☐
g I don't think there is any more to be said on this. ☐

4 Complete the action points from the meeting using the words and phrases from the box.

| back office | circulate | evening | look for | look into | property |

1 Try to find shopping centre locations for the branches in List B and contact _____ agencies.

2 _____ bank redesign specialists, preferably ones that can do _____ and weekend building work.

3 _____ market research data about what customers expect from a bank.

4 Find out what facilities the _____ staff want.

5 _____ the minutes by Wednesday.

5 Listen to check your answers, and then say who is responsible for each action point – Claire, Kirsten, Julie, John or Alan. **⊘12**

Writing

Finish the email below with information from **Questions 3** and **4**.

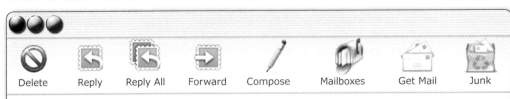

Date:
From: Pat Brady
To: John.Henry@ ..., Julie.Hoyte@ ..., Alan.Walcott@ ... Claire.Connolly@ ...
Cc: Kirsten.Olson@ ...
Subject: Action points from yesterday's meeting

Kirsten will be circulating the minutes of yesterday's meeting shortly, but meanwhile, here's a summary of the action points and who is responsible for them.

-
-
-
-

Practice 2

As you heard in the listening exercises in **Unit 10**, the National Union Bank in London is considering moving its telephone banking operations to India. This would involve closing down its call centre in Britain, and working with a company in India.

The telephone answering companies in India employ university graduates who speak English as a second language, but who earn much less than call centre staff in Britain. Even though the bank would have to pay for long-distance telephone calls (the British customers would still pay a local rate), it could save a lot of money by working with an Indian company.

The bank is having a meeting to decide whether to do this. At the moment there is no consensus: some people are for the idea and others are against.

Your teacher will give you a role to prepare. Use the phrases for expressing opinions, agreeing and disagreeing from the **Language focus**.

Work in groups of five. Student A should look at **page 119**, Student B at **page 128**, Student C at **page 135**, Student D at **page 133**, and Student E at **page 122**.

13 Foreign exchange

To learn about: exchange rates; foreign exchange trading; key vocabulary
  of exchange rates
To learn how to: talk about graphs and charts
To practise: describing a graph related to your work

Lead in

- How many different currencies can you name?
- How is the value (the exchange rate) of your currency determined?
- Has the exchange rate, compared to the US dollar or the euro, remained constant over the last few years?
- Do you know the history of your currency over the past 50 years?

Reading 1: Exchange rates

Look at the timeline below, showing key dates in the development of exchange rate systems around the world. Match the dates with the events (a–e) below.

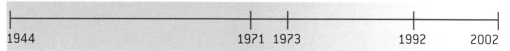

1944   1971 1973   1992   2002

a Most industrialized countries switched to a system of floating rates. However, governments and central banks occasionally attempted to influence exchange rates by intervening in the markets. So there was a system of managed floating exchange rates.

b The Bank of England lost over £5 billion in one day attempting to protect the value of the pound sterling. After this, governments and central banks intervened much less, so there was almost a freely floating system.

c A fixed exchange rate system was started. The values of many major currencies were pegged (or fixed) to the value of the US dollar. The American central bank, the Federal Reserve, guaranteed that it could exchange an ounce of gold for $35.

d Twelve states of the European Union introduced a single currency, the euro, to replace their national currencies.

e Gold convertibility ended because the Federal Reserve no longer had enough gold to back the dollar, due to inflation.

Listening: Freely floating exchange rates

1 Listen to Peter Sinclair talking about the potential problems of freely floating exchange rates, and answer the questions. ⊘13

    1 What does Sinclair say is the current trend in exchange rates?
    2 What examples does he give of unexpected pieces of news?
    3 What can happen to currencies in response to unexpected news?
    4 Why can currencies be at the wrong level for long periods of time?

2 Now listen again, and complete the last part of what Sinclair says. ⊘13

... a lot of the people who are operating in foreign exchange markets don't tend to think so much about (1) _____ _____ _____ and what the currency really ought to be (2) _____ in order for its goods to be (3) _____ at the right level in (4) _____ _____ and so on. They're trying to guess very (5) _____ _____ _____ , and they're trying to guess the (6) _____ of other traders. They tend to say, 'Oh, let's see, if something is going up today it will probably go up tomorrow.' They just go in one direction and you often get huge (7) _____ _____ _____ , going on for maybe even years, certainly for weeks and months, which are pushing the currency away from what it really ought to be. This is a source of (8) _____ and it's undoubtedly happening and it's due to the fact that people don't have (9) _____ _____ and often tend to say, 'Well, if he's doing this then he must know something I don't, I'd better copy him', and that can be a (10) _____ for real trouble.

3 Do you know any other words that could be used for answers (6) and (10)?

Discussion

- Has the value of the currency of your country risen or fallen in the past few weeks or months? Do you know why?
- What international events do you expect to affect exchange rates in the next few weeks or months? Why and how?
- How could you attempt to profit from these changes, if you had a large amount of cash at your disposal?

Reading 2: Currency trading

1 You are going to read a text about online currency trading. Before you read, answer the following questions.

    1 Why do people buy and sell currencies?
    2 What do you think the world's seven major currencies are?

2 Now read the text and – using your own words as much as possible – write seven statements about the following figures:

a	5%	e	1,000,000,000,000
b	30	f	24
c	85%	g	95%
d	2		

MGS — FX Trading

http://www.mgsbank.com/fx

The Foreign Exchange market, also referred to as the 'Forex' or 'FX' market, is the largest financial market in the world, with a daily average turnover of well over US$1 trillion – 30 times larger than the combined volume of all U.S. equity markets.

Foreign Exchange is the simultaneous buying of one currency and selling of another. Currencies are traded in pairs, for example Euro/US Dollar (EUR/USD) or US Dollar/Japanese Yen (USD/JPY).

There are two reasons to buy and sell currencies. About 5% of daily turnover is from companies and governments that buy or sell products and services in a foreign country or must convert profits made in foreign currencies into their domestic currency. The other 95% is trading for profit, or speculation.

For speculators, the best trading opportunities are with the most commonly traded (and therefore most liquid) currencies, called 'the Majors'. Today, more than 85% of all daily transactions involve trading of the Majors, which include the US Dollar, Japanese Yen, Euro, British Pound, Swiss Franc, Canadian Dollar and Australian Dollar.

A true 24-hour market, Forex trading begins each day in Sydney, and moves around the globe as the business day begins in each financial center, first to Tokyo, London, and New York. Unlike any other financial market, investors can respond to currency fluctuations caused by economic, social and political events at the time they occur – day or night.

The FX market is considered an Over The Counter (OTC) or 'interbank' market, due to the fact that transactions are conducted between two counterparts over the telephone or via an electronic network. Trading is not centralized on an exchange, as with the stock and futures markets.

3   Find the words in the text that mean the following:

1   the total amount of money spent in a market
2   another word for stocks and shares
3   belonging to one's own country
4   people who buy and sell things in the hope of making a profit
5   easy to sell (to convert into cash)
6   price changes

Describing trends and graphs

If we want to show changes in the value of a currency, trends in the economy or any other quantities which change over time, we often use graphs. There are a number of commonly used words and phrases to describe upward and downward movement, as well as the rate and size of the change.

1   The phrases in the box are used to describe trends and graphs. Put them in the table below, according to the word category. One has been done for you.

dramatic increase	gradual rise	rapid decline
fall sharply	level off	slight drop
gradually decrease	moderate growth	sudden climb

	→	↘	⟶		Speed	Size
Verbs		*fall*		Adjectives		
Nouns				Adverbs	*sharply*	

2   Do you know any other words and phrases that can be added to the table?

3 Look at the graph showing the development of the USD / GBP exchange rate and complete the description using words and phrases from the box.

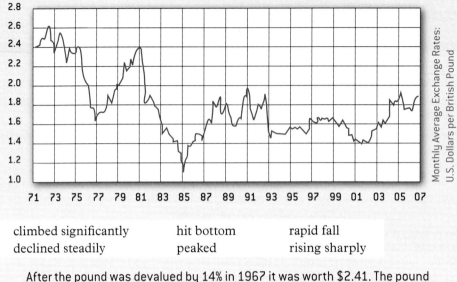

Monthly Average Exchange Rates:
U.S. Dollars per British Pound

| climbed significantly | hit bottom | rapid fall |
| declined steadily | peaked | rising sharply |

After the pound was devalued by 14% in 1967 it was worth $2.41. The pound floated after 1971, and (1) _____ during 1975 and 1976, before (2) _____ again between 1977 and 1980. There was a (3) _____ in 1981, and the pound continued to slide until 1985, when it (4) _____ at $1.06. In 1991 it reached $1.88, and (5) _____ at $1.96 in 1990, but in 1993 it fell again to below $1.50. The pound (6) _____ again during most of 2002–3.

4 Add any new words from the exercise to the table on **page 65**.

Practice

Find a graph from your job, a business publication or on the internet, and the necessary background information. Then explain it to the class using some of the words from the **Language focus**, and answer any questions they have. (If you can't find a graph but you have the information, you could produce the graph yourself.)
For example, you could explain:

- changes in the sales of a product
- changes in the cash flow produced by an investment
- changes in economic indicators such as unemployment, inflation or interest rates
- changes in real estate values or house prices
- share price performance
- company performance (sales, profits, etc.), to assess the risk of lending it money
- market conditions and demographic trends, in relation to marketing and sales planning for a new product.

14 Writing reports 1

AIMS

To learn how to: structure reports; separate facts and opinions; give findings, recommendations and examples; use connectors
To practise: writing a report on online trade finance

Lead in

- Do you have to read reports or long documents? Are they usually well written?
- What kind of reports or long documents do you have to write?
- Who do you write them for? How does this affect their content and the style?

Discussion

In which order would the following parts normally come in a long report?

☐ Appendix or appendices: for tables, figures, etc.

☐ Conclusions: based on the facts and alternatives

☐ Contents list: including headings and sub-headings with page numbers

☐ Introduction: stating the report's aims or objectives, or its terms of reference (why it was written and who it was written for)

☐ Recommendations: the action the writer thinks should be taken based on the facts, discussion and conclusions

☐ Summary: giving the main points, such as important conclusions

☐ The main part of the report: giving and discussing the facts and findings, and perhaps considering alternative courses of action

☐ Title page: giving the subject, the writer's name, the date and (if necessary) a reference number

Reading: Facts and opinions

1 Read the extract from a report written by the Head of Retail Operations of MGS Bank about the future of their branches (see **Unit 3**) and decide whether the statements (1–11) on **page 68** are facts or opinions.

A market research survey of over 2,700 customers conducted for one of our competitors showed that 52% of them prefer using a bank branch to using the telephone or the internet. It also showed that 45% of customers in the richer AB social group – the customers I feel we should be particularly interested in – also preferred to use bank branches. I believe this is also true of younger customers, the ones you'd expect to use the internet.

I have the feeling that younger customers are also more likely to be responsive to the design of the branches, so I think we should test sample designs with younger customers.

Research has demonstrated that well-designed branches attract more customers, who then buy more banking products, but location and staffing are also important. It seems to me that opening new branches in shopping centres would soon become profitable, despite the high rents. Some of our competitors now have coffee shops in the bank; this is something we should copy, in my view. Having friendly staff behind the counter is also extremely important, and I'm inclined to think that a small percentage of our staff need some training in this respect.

We also have a lot of data revealing that our customers – though not our staff – want us to open longer hours, until 6 pm from Monday to Friday, and on Saturday mornings. We will have to start negotiating with the staff about this.

1   A majority of retail bank customers prefer to use a bank branch.
2   Forty-five per cent of more wealthy customers prefer to use bank branches.
3   MGS Bank should be more interested in customers in the AB social group.
4   Younger customers also prefer going to branches to using the internet.
5   Younger customers are more responsive to bank design.
6   MGS Bank should test sample designs with younger customers.
7   Well-designed branches attract more customers, who buy more products.
8   It could be profitable to open branches in shopping centres.
9   MGS Bank should open small coffee shops in its branches.
10 Some of MGS Bank's staff require training in being friendly to customers.
11 Customers want MGS Bank to extend its opening hours.

2 Now read the text again and underline the words used to give opinions.

Useful phrases

To give recommendations, rather than opinions, we use phrases introducing actions.

> *We should …*
> *We ought to …*
> *We must …*   (stronger than *should* or *ought to*)
> *I strongly recommend …*
> *It would be advisable to …*   (impersonal; it's not <u>you</u> advising it)

Writing 1

The author of the report in the **Reading** exercise does not separate facts (e.g. from market research surveys) from his own opinions. A report should usually present the findings (the results of the research) and then the recommendations, which follow logically from the writer's opinions.

Rewrite the report extract from the exercise above in two sections, the first giving the findings and the second giving recommendations. Use the **Useful phrases** above for your recommendations.

Linking words

When writing a report it is important to connect your ideas logically and effectively, but without always using the same words and phrases. Match the groups of conjunctions and connectors (1–8) to their uses (a–f). Some uses can be matched to more than one group.

1 for example, for instance, such as
We need to find out what new facilities the back office staff would like, *such as* computer upgrades, on-site parking facilities.

2 also, furthermore, moreover
When writing a report you should separate facts and opinions. *Furthermore*, you should make sure your opinions are supported by your findings.

3 in other words, i.e.
This applies to a lot of customers in the AB social group, *i.e.* customers with higher incomes who the bank is particularly interested in.

4 because, since, as (followed by a clause with a subject and a verb)
Some customers don't bank online *as* they are worried about security.

5 because of, due to, owing to (followed by a noun or noun phrase)
Our profits fell *due to* increased competition.

6 consequently, therefore, thus, as a result
Some customers are worried about internet security. *Consequently*, they don't want to do online banking.

7 though, although, even though, while
(used in either the first or second clause of a contrast)
Even though rents are high, branches in shopping centres are profitable.

Branches in shopping centres are profitable *even though* rents are high.

8 however, on the other hand, yet, on the contrary
(used in the second clause or sentence of a contrast)
Branches in shopping centres are expensive. *Yet* they attract a lot of customers.

Renting property in shopping centres isn't cheap. *On the contrary*, it's extremely expensive.

a To clarify (to express something already said or written in different words)
b To express consequences
c To express contrast
d To express reasons and causes
e To give a second or third argument or example
f To give an example of something that has just been mentioned

Vocabulary

1 The Head of Internet Banking at MGS Bank wants to put a large amount of information about the bank's services on the internet, to provide information to companies involved in importing and exporting, and to enable companies to arrange finance online. Read the beginning of the report.

Introduction

This report, written by Jay Green, Head of Internet Banking, to be submittedto the Chief Executive, recommends setting up a separate trade finance website and introducing online trade finance facilities.

Given the success of online banking in our Retail Banking department, this report will recommend extending online banking to our trade finance services. The Trade Finance department could have its own website providing information to companies involved in importing and exporting. It could include standardized application forms for letters of credit and bills of exchange, giving customers the possibility to start transactions and deliver instructions online.

2 The next part of the report gives further reasons for setting up a specialized website and offering online trade finance services, and discusses the advantages and disadvantages of the proposal. The sentences (1–8) below are from this part of the report. Choose the correct conjunctions or connectors from the brackets to complete the sentences. Look at the **Language focus** to help you.

1 Most banks do not offer this service: (yet / moreover, / on the contrary,) very few do, which is why this would give us a big advantage.

2 A lot of small companies are frightened to import directly (because / owing to / although) the complexity of documentary credits.

3 This service would be particularly useful for 'dotcom' start-ups – (therefore / for example, / in other words,) new internet companies – who want to buy and sell internationally.

4 (Although / Consequently, / As) there would be initial costs in setting up the website, it would subsequently save us a lot of money.

5 (Furthermore, / Such as / On the other hand,) offering these services would probably gain us a lot of new customers.

6 (Moreover, / Because of / Though) it would reduce our costs and make each transaction more profitable, (also / since / due to) the customer would be doing a lot of the work online – (while / though / for instance,) filling in the details on a letter of credit.

7 (Yet / As a result, / Since) we might no longer need some of the staff processing customer instructions.

8 (Even though / However, / Thus,) these staff could almost certainly be transferred to other departments.

Writing 2

Write a report about setting up a trade finance website, following on from the Introduction above. The report should continue with the main part (the author's findings), followed by the conclusions and recommendations. Information on what the author considers to be the advantages of setting up such a website is given in the **Vocabulary** exercise above. Do <u>not</u> copy these sentences exactly, but rewrite them, keeping the same facts or arguments.

The information and facilities the Head of Internet Banking wants to put online include:

- a list of the bank's trade finance products and services
- information about import and export risks
- information about trade financing options, including letters of credit and bills of exchange
- product diagrams (flow charts) demonstrating how letters of credit and bills of exchange work
- application forms for letters of credit, bills of exchange and other forms of payment
- information about Incoterms
- information about trade insurance
- details about the bank's fees
- answers to frequently asked questions.

Remember, your purpose is to convince the bank (beginning with the Chief Executive, and then the Head of Trade Finance) to set up a trade finance website, and online trade finance facilities. Before writing, think about the background information they need, and how you will organize and structure the information. After writing, make sure that you check the grammar and spelling thoroughly, and ensure that your conclusions and recommendations are clear.

15 Stocks and shares

AIMS

To learn about: stocks and shares; key vocabulary of the stock market
To learn how to: talk about market price changes
To practise: describing changes in share prices

The New York Times

"All the News That's Fit to Print"

Late Edition
New York: Today, increasing clouds. High 62-67. Tonight, cloudy, breezy, showers likely. Low 51-57. Tomorrow, showers ending. High 58-63. Yesterday: High 68, low 48. Details on page B6.

VOL.CXXXVII... No. 47,298   Copyright © 1987 The New York Times   NEW YORK, TUESDAY, OCTOBER 20, 19   30 CENTS

STOCKS PLUNGE 508 POINTS, A DROP OF 22.6%

'October. This is one of the peculiarly dangerous months to speculate in stocks in. The others are July, January, September, April, November, May, March, June, December, August and February.'

Mark Twain (1894)

Discussion

- Have you ever speculated in anything? What happened?
- Do you agree with Mark Twain that it's always dangerous to speculate in stocks and shares?
- There were two big stock market crashes in the twentieth century. Do you know when?
- Do you know why and how companies issue shares?
- Do you possess any shares? Why did you buy them? How did you buy them?

Vocabulary 1

You are going to read about share prices. Before you read, check your understanding of the words and phrases in the box by matching them with their definitions (1–10).

bankruptcy	bubble	collateral	institutional investors	raise capital
bears	bulls	day traders	issue	shares

1 a name for investors who buy shares because they expect their price to rise
2 a name for shareholders who sell because they expect the price to fall
3 a period of rapidly rising share prices, followed by a quick collapse
4 assets a borrower uses to secure or guarantee a loan
5 certificates representing part-ownership of a company
6 financial organizations that own a lot of shares
7 people who buy and re-sell shares in a very short time, often just a few hours
8 to get money from investors with which to run a business
9 to offer securities for sale, to financial institutions and the public
10 when you have no money to pay your debts, so you have to sell your assets

Reading: Why stock markets matter

1 Can you think of any ways that changes in share prices could affect people who don't own any shares themselves?

2 Now read the text and compare it with the answers you gave to **Question 1**.

NEWS

Why stock markets matter for you *Stefan Armbruster, BBC News online*

The saying goes: 'Don't invest what you can't afford to lose'.

But as stock markets fall, it is not just people who own shares who lose out. When the bears replace the bulls – in other words, when the market falls – it affects almost everyone because stocks and shares have become an integral part of almost all our financial lives.

There are a variety of ways in which stock market movements impact on our lives. The upbeat side of the growth in share ownership is that when the stock market goes up, consumers with shares feel richer, they borrow more and they spend more. But just as the stock market can go up, it can also go down. Usually the first to react to this are the institutional investors who are involved in the financial markets on a daily basis.

The internet boom is an example. Many personal investors felt they were burnt by the popping of the dot.com bubble. By the time they got around to selling shares in any number of failing internet based companies, the big City investors had already pulled out of the market. The institutional investors did not escape unharmed either. And the hits that they took also have an indirect, but potentially serious, effect on many people's financial health. Any pain suffered by these institutional investors impacts on the returns paid on pensions, savings accounts or the interest charged on mortgages.

For individuals with a more direct interest – say day traders attracted by the tech boom – share holdings can be used as collateral to borrow money. But if the value and income from shares evaporate and the bank calls in the loan, the result can be big losses or personal bankruptcy. Meanwhile pensions linked to the stock market, like the ones being promoted by the UK government, are not immune. Unlike the state pension which is paid out at a rate set by the government, investing in a private pension indexed to the stock market can increase the value of the contributions dramatically, but they can also be erased.

Your job can also depend on the markets as companies use their valuation and the issue of new shares to raise capital to expand. If they are unable to do this then they have to find ways of increasing the company's value to attract investors. The key tool they use is to cut jobs. ▶

3 According to the text, are the following statements true or false?

1 Nearly everybody suffers the consequences when share prices go down.
2 Institutional investors are usually slower to sell when the market falls than personal investors.
3 The value of pensions paid by the government can go up and down with the stock market.
4 Companies can acquire new capital for expansion by issuing new shares.
5 Companies sometimes make people redundant in order to increase the company's value (and its share price).

Vocabulary 2

1 The phrases in the box have different meanings according to the situation they are used in. What meaning do they have in the text?

a to lose money   b not to lose money

    to be burnt   to suffer pain
    to escape unharmed   to take a hit

2 Find phrases in the text that mean the following:

    1 to sell all your stocks
    2 to demand that a loan is repaid
    3 to encourage people or companies to buy shares
    4 to fire people

LANGUAGE FOCUS

Understanding market reports

1 In **Unit 13**, you looked at some words and phrases for describing trends and graphs, such as *increase*, *decrease* and *level off*. In order to make financial reports more varied and interesting, financial journalists use a wide range of words and phrases to describe different movements in the markets. The language they use is often more dramatic and colourful in order to attract your attention. Can you think of any examples of this kind of language which you have seen or heard recently?

2 Look at the following headlines and decide what type of movement they are describing. Then put the words and phrases in the table below. You will add more later.

Oil prices rally after Monday's fall

IT stocks take a beating; strong rupee blamed

Stocks stage another comeback

Chinese stocks take a tumble

Telecom goes through the roof

Global coffee prices under pressure

Boeing sees quarterly profits slide

To go up	To go down	To stay the same

3 Listen to the financial market report from the radio news. Have the following prices gone up ↑, gone down ↓, or stayed the same ↔? The first one has been done as an example. *15*

1 Stocks in Japan   ↑

2 Stocks in France

3 France Telecom

4 Thomson

5 Stocks in Germany

6 Lufthansa

7 Stocks in Britain

8 British Energy

9 Vodafone

10 Copper

11 Gold

12 Silver

4 Listen to the market report again, and add the words and phrases to the table on **page 73**. Can you add any other verbs? *15*

Practice 1

You are going to describe a graph to a partner, and draw your partner's graph from a description. Your teacher will give you a role to prepare. Use the words and phrases from the **Language focus**. You can also use language from **Unit 13**.

Work in pairs. Student A should look at **page 119**, and Student B at **page 128**.

Practice 2

In pairs or groups, select 10 different stocks or shares, and invest an imaginary €10,000 in them, dividing up the sum as you wish. You can choose companies on any major stock exchange, but remember that if you buy shares in foreign currencies there is a risk of exchange rate movements.

Choose several blue chips – shares in large, well-established companies with a good reputation for quality and profitability – as well as two high-tech companies, and two companies that have only been listed or quoted on the stock exchange for less than a year (this information can be found in the financial pages of newspapers).

Follow the progress of your portfolio in the financial press or on the internet. Depending on the length of your course, select a date to report back, and see whose portfolio has gained the most value – or lost the least!

16 Writing reports 2

To learn how to: use the right style and tone; use the right presentation and layout
To practise: writing a complete report

Lead in

- How long has your company been in its current location?
- What sort of amenities does your building have – for example, parking, a canteen? Are they adequate?
- What sort of things would your company look for in a new building, if it wanted to relocate?

Reading: Head office relocation

Metropolis Bank is a large American full service bank, formed from the merger of a commercial bank with an investment bank, a private bank and an insurance company. It is moving all its departments, which are currently in a number of different locations in New York City, to a new corporate headquarters in the financial district in downtown Manhattan.

Eight thousand staff will be relocated to a new, 40-storey high-rise building, which is currently being designed. The bank has circulated a questionnaire asking staff about what facilities they would like in the new building (without, of course, guaranteeing that all choices and requests can be accommodated).

The questionnaire included the following questions:

STAFF Questionnaire

▶ **Eating**
- Do you prefer to eat out at lunchtime or stay in?

- Do you normally eat lunch with colleagues or alone?

- If eating in, what style of facility would you prefer in the new building – cafeteria, restaurant, snack bar, sandwich shop, coffee shops?

- Would you bring your own lunch? Hot or cold? What kind of facilities would you require in the new building for storing and consuming food?

▶ **Exercise**
- Would you use on-site leisure facilities, such as a gym, an exercise class, and squash or basketball courts?

▶ **Health care**
- Would you use an on-site doctor or dentist?

- Would you need travel advice and inoculations?

▶ **Travel to work**
- Do you need motorbike or cycle parking, and changing facilities? (Car parking is unfortunately not an option.)

There was also space for raising concerns, making requests and expressing other preferences.

Discussion

- If you worked for this bank, how would you answer the questionnaire?
- How do the proposed facilities compare with the ones you have where you work or study?
- Is there anything else you would expect the bank to propose?
- Do you, or would you like to, work in a large or a small organization? In a large headquarters or a small department? What are the advantages and disadvantages of each?

Listening 1: Catering choices

1 You will hear the human resources manager responsible for collating the questionnaire responses talking with the relocation Project Manager. Listen and answer the following questions. ⊘ **16.1**

   1 Why is the HR manager surprised about the number of responses?
   2 How many days a week do most staff eat in their office building?
   3 How many people usually bring their own food to work?
   4 What is the capacity of the planned restaurant?

2 Listen again and make notes about what the staff want. You will use these notes later to write a report. ⊘ **16.1**

Listening 2: Health and leisure needs

1 Listen to the rest of the conversation between the HR manager and the Project Manager, and answer the following questions. ⊘ **16.2**

   1 There are two staff requests that are impossible to meet. They are consequently irrelevant, and do not need to be included in the report. What are they?
   2 Which of the exercise and leisure facilities proposed in the questionnaire do the staff seem to want?
   3 Why do most staff seem not to want medical treatment at work?
   4 One hundred people made the same request. What is it?
   5 What is the special booklet the HR manager plans to send everybody, and why?
   6 What else is worrying a lot of people about the new headquarters?

2 Listen again and make notes about what the staff want, and what they don't want. You will use these notes later to write a report.

Writing 1

1 In pairs or groups, compare your lists of the things the staff do and do not want, and make a definitive list you agree on.

2 Now write an Introduction stating the report's Terms of Reference (see **Unit 14**).

3 Then write a brief Outline of the whole report, giving the main points and conclusions. This will provide a framework for writing the whole report. It will also be the basis of the Summary, which will appear at the beginning of the report, even if it is not the first thing to be written.

   Keep these documents, as you will later write a complete report, containing findings, conclusions and recommendations.

Style and tone

You have heard the Project Manager and the HR manager having a relaxed and fairly casual conversation. A written report would obviously use a different, more formal kind of language. But there are also different ways of writing a report, and different levels of formality, depending on its purpose and who it is for.

Look at the following two documents and answer the questions:

1 Who do you think they were written for?
2 What kind of language are they written in?
3 What elements do they contain that you would not use in a report for senior management?

a

BUSINESS NEWS

Next summer Metropolis Bank is moving to a new 40-storey headquarters building in the Financial District, designed by award-winning architects Godwin-Malone.

The breathtaking 700-foot tower, built with all the latest cutting-edge technology, has four basement levels and 40 floors providing over a million square feet of

office space. The building consists of 13,500 tons of steel, 175,000 tons of concrete, and 450,900 square feet of glass. It will provide a state-of-the-art working environment for 8,000 employees. Facilities for staff will include an 850-seat staff restaurant – one of the largest of its kind in the world – that will serve over 2,500 meals a day. The basement levels will include a fully equipped multi-purpose gymnasium with high-tech cardio and weight-training machines, and rooms for a full range of exercise classes (aerobics, yoga and Pilates). Staff will be offered personal training programs according to their individual needs, designed by top-notch qualified trainers.

b

| Delete | Reply | Reply All | Forward | Compose | Mailboxes | Get Mail | Junk |

Hi there

Well, we've finally got the results back from the questionnaire and there are a few surprises – like some people want a swimming pool – can you believe it?!

Tons of people want a restaurant for breakfast and lunch, and lots wanted coffee and sandwich shops too. Loads of people, especially the women, want gym and exercise classes but there's not much call for squash or basketball courts.

Surprisingly, hardly anyone wanted doctors or dentists on site – worries about confidentiality, I think, so we can cross that one out.

The 'picnic people' want fridges and microwaves, and there are a lot of cyclists who want cycle parking and somewhere to change.

And, one last surprise – some people want a convenience store – I mean, they're supposed to be working, not shopping!

The good news is that most of this is already planned, so we can get straight down to business.

That's it for now!

Writing 2

1   One of the features of the first text is its use of subjective adjectives, such as *breathtaking*, which show the writer's opinion and often have the effect of exaggerating. Look at the text and underline all of the subjective adjectives. Then rewrite it as a short factual report, removing the subjective adjectives and the less important details.

2   In pairs, rewrite the second text as a short factual report, removing some of the informal expressions. Keep this document ready for your full report.

Writing 3

Write a complete report, to be submitted to the Board of Directors, containing a summary of the questionnaire responses (but also taking into account what has already been planned), as well as recommendations as to which facilities to provide in the new building.

The list of questions in the **Reading** activity (or a copy of the actual questionnaire) would usually be included as an Appendix.

Remember that even a well-written report will look bad if it has a bad layout.

Some basic recommendations:

- Use clear headings and sub-headings.
- Use the same spacing throughout the document.
- Use only one font, or two at the most, with bold font for emphasis.
- Write in short and focused sections.

As examples, look at the documents included in companies' published Annual Reports.

17 Mergers and acquisitions

AIMS

To learn about: mergers and acquisitions; key vocabulary of mergers, takeovers and buyouts

To learn how to: talk about cause and effect

To practise: talking about the effects of takeovers

Mittal in £13bn hostile bid for Arcelor

Arcelor to merge with Russian steel group

UK acquisitions already worth $66bn this year

eBay snaps up PayPal for £1bn

Corporate raiders making a comeback

Google gobbles up YouTube in $1.65bn takeover

After GE acquisition, Swiss Re says 2,000 jobs to go

Lead in

- What is a merger?
- What is a takeover?
- What is a takeover bid?
- What is a raid?
- What is a friendly takeover?
- What is a hostile takeover?
- Why do companies merge?
- Why do companies buy other companies?
- Think of a recent merger or takeover that was reported in the press: what were the reasons behind it?

Reading: Mergers, takeovers and buyouts

Read the text on page 80 and match the titles (1–5) to the paragraphs (a–e).

1 Disadvantages of takeovers ☐
2 Raiders and asset-stripping ☐
3 Raids and bids ☐
4 The 'make-or-buy' decision ☐
5 The role of banks ☐

"I'm feeling absolutely marvelous.
I think I'll acquire another company."

a Successful companies generally want to diversify: to introduce new products or services, and enter new markets. Yet entering new markets with new brands is usually a slow, expensive and risky process, so buying another company with existing products and customers is often cheaper and safer. If a company is too big to acquire, another possibility is to merge with it, forming a new company out of the two old ones. Apart from diversifying, reasons for acquiring companies include getting a stronger position in a market and a larger market share, reducing competition, benefiting from economies of scale, and making better use of plant and equipment.

b There are two ways to acquire a company: a raid and a takeover bid. A raid simply involves buying as many of a company's stocks as possible on the stock market. Of course if there is more demand for stock than there are sellers, this increases the stock price. A takeover bid is a public offer to a company's stockholders to buy their stocks at a certain price (higher than the current market price) during a limited period of time. This can be much more expensive than a raid, because if all the stockholders accept the bid, the buyer has to purchase 100% of the company's stocks, even though they only need 50% plus one to gain control of a company. (In fact they often need much less, as many stockholders do not vote at stockholders' meetings.) If stockholders accept a bid, but receive stocks in the other company instead of cash, it is not always clear if the operation is a takeover or a merger – journalists sometimes use both terms.

c Companies are sometimes encouraged to take over other ones by investment banks, if researchers in their Mergers and Acquisitions departments consider that the target companies are undervalued. Banks can earn high fees for advising on takeovers.

d Yet there are also a number of good arguments *against* takeovers. Diversification can damage a company's image, goodwill and shared values (e.g. quality, good service, innovation). After a hostile takeover (when the managers of a company do not want it to be taken over), the top executives of the newly acquired company are often replaced or choose to leave. This is a problem if what made the company special was its staff (or 'human capital') rather than its products or customer base. Furthermore, a company's optimum size or market share can be quite small, and large conglomerates can become unmanageable and inefficient. Takeovers do not always result in synergy. In fact, statistics show that most mergers and acquisitions reduce rather than increase the company's value.

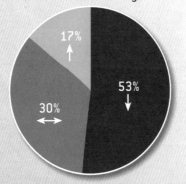

Stockholder value: was the company's stock price higher 12 months after the merger or acquisition, compared with the overall trend for the industry?

A survey of the 700 largest international merger and acquisition deals during a three-year period showed the following:

In 17% the deal created value.
In 30% the deal neither created nor destroyed value.
In 53% the deal destroyed value.

e Consequently, corporate raiders and private equity companies look for large conglomerates (formed by a series of takeovers) which have become inefficient, and so are undervalued. In other words, their market capitalization (the price of all their stocks) is less than the value of their total assets, including land, buildings and – unfortunately – pension funds. Raiders can borrow money, usually by issuing bonds, and buy the companies. They then split them up or sell off the assets, and then pay back the bonds while making a large profit. Until the law was changed, they were also able to appropriate the pension funds. This is known as asset-stripping, and such takeovers are called leveraged buyouts or LBOs. If a company's own managers buy its stocks, this is a management buyout or MBO.

Vocabulary

Find words or phrases in the text that mean the following:

1 adding new and different products or services
2 a company's sales expressed as a percentage of the total sales in a market
3 reductions in costs resulting from increased production
4 money paid to investment banks for work done
5 all the individuals or organizations that regularly or occasionally purchase goods or services from a company
6 best, perfect or ideal (adjective)
7 combined production or productivity that is greater than the sum of the separate parts
8 people or companies that try to buy and sell other companies to make a profit
9 large corporations or groups of companies offering a number of different products or services
10 buying a company in order to sell its most valuable assets at a profit

Listening: The role of banks

1 You are going to listen to Peter Sinclair talking about the role of banks in mergers and takeovers. Before you listen, check your understanding of the words and phrases (1–5) below by matching them with their definitions (a–e).

1 a buying spree
2 boom
3 cyclical (adjective)
4 slump
5 to drum up business

a a period when an economy is doing badly
b buying a lot in a short period
c to try to get new customers
d a period when an economy is doing very well
e going round and round or repeating

2 Now listen, and look at the following statements. Are they true or false, according to Peter Sinclair? 🔘17

1 Investment banks sometimes encourage companies to acquire other ones, because this creates business for the bank.
2 The acquisitions policy of well-managed companies can be influenced by banks.
3 There are more takeovers when share prices are high.
4 Share prices were high all through the 1980s and 1990s.
5 When share prices are high, investment banks tell companies what to buy.
6 A company that doesn't want to be taken over will get advice from a large financial institution such as an investment bank.
7 The value of merchant banks has recently gone down.

Cause and effect

When talking about takeovers, Peter Sinclair uses words that link a cause and an effect: 'companies feel richer ... *so* they tend to go out on a buying spree', and '... boom for shares *means* more takeovers'.

Here are some other linking words and expressions that can be used to describe cause and effect:

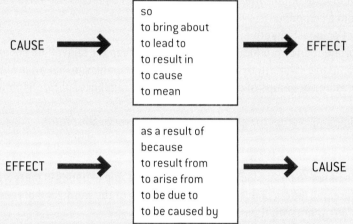

Examples:
I was offered a better job in a bank *so* I left the insurance company.
Deregulation *brought about* major changes in the financial industry.
Major changes *have arisen from* the deregulation of the financial industry.

Look at the sentences about Procter & Gamble and Gillette, and make new sentences describing cause and effect.

28 January 2005: Procter & Gamble announces that it is going to buy Gillette for $57 billion.

28 January 2005: Gillette rises nearly 13% on Wall Street, while P&G drops 2.1%.

P&G predicts cost savings of between $14 billion and $16 billion from economies of scale and restructuring of the two companies. The combined companies' sales will be over $60 billion a year.

10 April 2005: The US Federal Trade Commission (FTC) approves the acquisition, as long as the companies divest some overlapping product lines, so as to restore competition in the market.

July 2005: Shareholders of both companies approve the proposed merger.

July 2005: The European Union approves the merger, as long as P&G sells its line of battery-operated toothbrushes.

1 October 2005: The purchase is finalized. P&G exchanges its common stock for Gillette stock. Gillette shareholders get an 18% premium on the closing share prices of 27 January 2005.

The Gillette Company ceases to exist and its stocks are no longer traded.

P&G becomes the world's biggest household goods maker.

6,000 people, 4% of the combined workforce of 140,000, lose their jobs because of overlaps in management and business support functions.

January 2006: P&G announces a 27% increase in sales and a 29% increase in net earnings.

Practice 1

Take the graph you described in **Unit 13**, and describe it to your partner, using the words and phrases to describe cause and effect from the **Language focus** opposite. Do not let your partner see your graph. Then draw the graph that your partner describes to you, and ask him or her to explain the rises and falls.

Practice 2

MGS, a regional commercial bank with 30 branches offering a range of financial services to local businesses and private individuals, is facing a takeover bid by a much larger national competitor. The small size of the bank and the continuing trend of consolidation in the retail banking sector make it likely that the bank will sooner or later lose its independence.

The executive directors of the bank are going to have a meeting to decide what to recommend to the shareholders. Your teacher will give you a role to prepare. In the meeting, use the words and phrases to describe cause and effect from the **Language focus** opposite.

Work in groups of five. Student A should look at **page 119**, Student B at **page 129**, Student C at **page 135**, Student D at **page 133**, and Student E at **page 122**.

Writing

Write a short summary of the meeting to send to the Board, giving your decision and explaining the reasons for it. You may want to look back at **Unit 12** for language to report opinions.

18 Negotiating 1

To learn how to: negotiate; make, accept and reject proposals, counter-proposals and conditional offers

To practise: making conditional offers and negotiating the conditions of a commercial loan

Lead in

- Are you a good negotiator ?
- In what circumstances do you have to negotiate in your everyday life?
- In what circumstances do you have to negotiate at work, both formally (in meetings) and informally (just talking with colleagues)?
- What skills and qualities do you think a good negotiator has?
- Can you learn these skills, or must you be born with them?

© 2003 Ted Goff

GOFF

"Let's start the negotiations with you taking 99.99% off the price."

Vocabulary

You are going to read about negotiating. Before you read, check your understanding of the words and phrases (1–10) below by matching them with their definitions (a–j).

1	compromise	a	a description of a possible event in the future
2	concession	b	a useful piece of information or advice
3	counter-proposal	c	an agreement that settles an argument when people reduce their demands in order to agree
4	deal point	d	an exchange involving giving up one thing to get something else
5	to leave something hanging	e	an individual item or element in a negotiation
6	parameters	f	an offer responding to somebody else's offer
7	scenario	g	fixed limits within which something can or must happen or be done
8	to set something aside	h	to delay making (or to forget to make) a decision about something
9	tip	i	to temporarily ignore or not think about a particular fact
10	trade-off	j	something which is accepted or given up by one side in order to end a disagreement

Reading: Learn to Love Negotiating

1 Read the text by Eric J. Adams, which gives advice about negotiating. Which of the negotiating tips do you think is the most difficult to put into practice?

The Art of Business: Learn to Love Negotiating

Business tips

Home | Archives | Directories | Services

Search ➡

A few tips.

Be prepared. Before you negotiate, know exactly what you want and be ready to articulate your position; a negotiating meeting is no place to figure out the terms that are acceptable to you. You won't get every deal point, but at least you'll know in advance what are your parameters. In fact, it helps to break down your concerns into three categories: nice to have, like to have, and must have. Walk through several 'what if' scenarios beforehand. Anticipate counter-proposals and compromises and think about how you will react to each.

Be inquisitive. Don't be shy about asking questions. Skilful questions can transform a negotiation from an adversarial conflict into a partnership. By asking questions, you'll also get your client to reveal more. Start with open-ended questions and move to narrower, more direct questions. Once you have asked a question, be quiet and listen carefully.

Avoid significant early concessions. At the very least, remain neutral to the customer's initial demands until trade-off opportunities emerge or your gentle attempts at persuasion don't work.

Be prepared for disagreement. There will be disagreement and disappointment during any negotiation. But how you disagree will affect the outcome and ultimately affect your relationship with the client. When you disagree, look for the common ground or set the point aside until later. At the end of your discussions, you may find you have four or five points of disagreement. You can then exchange deal-point concessions until all points of contention are dealt with.

Expect the unexpected. Always have a good idea in advance of how you'll respond if things do not work out as you plan.

Finalize all agreements. Don't leave details hanging. It is often amazing how two people sitting in the same room can have different perspectives concerning what was agreed upon. To ensure that everyone is clear, summarize the agreement verbally or shortly afterward in a letter of agreement.

2 Put the following elements of a typical negotiation into a logical order.

1☐   2☐   3☐   4☐   5☐

a   Listen carefully to what the other side says.
b   Make trade-offs: you concede something they want for something you want.
c   Decide what you want and determine your minimum requirements – what you must get
    if there is to be an agreement.
d   Think about acceptable compromises in relation to expected counter-proposals, and try
    to imagine the counter-proposals the other side will make.
e   Summarize, verbally or in writing, what has been agreed.

3 Which of these things are done before the actual negotiation begins?

Making proposals, counter-proposals and conditional offers

Making and accepting proposals

1 Think of some simple phrases for making proposals using the words from the box.

offer	prepared	proposal	propose

2 Here are some common phrases for accepting proposals, with their words in the wrong order. Rewrite them correctly, adding capital letters and punctuation where needed.

1 fine yes sounds that
2 be think would I acceptable yes that
3 agree can to we that
4 think go along can we with that I

Conditional offers and counter-proposals

In negotiations, the conditional form is often used to make alternative proposals or offers. These offers usually contain the word *if* or a phrase with a similar meaning. There are different grammatical structures for conditionals; the form you choose depends on your opinion of the situation.

3 Match each sentence to the situation it is used in.

1 *I'll lower the price if you pay cash.*
2 *I'd lower the price, if you paid cash.*
a The speaker thinks that the customer is likely to pay cash.
b The speaker thinks that the customer is unlikely to pay cash.

will (or *'ll*) + infinitive ... *if* + present tense means that the speaker thinks there is a good possibility that the thing will happen.

would (or *'d*) + infinitive ... *if* + past tense means that the speaker thinks the situation is improbable.

Sometimes *can*, *could* and *might* are used instead of *will* and *would*:

I *can* lower the price if you pay cash.
I *might* be able to do that if you order 500.
I *could* imagine working there if they paid me $200,000.

In negotiations, *would* is also sometimes used with the present tense:

I *would* agree to that if you *lower* the price.

Unless means *except if*:

I can't reduce the price *unless* you pay cash.
I wouldn't take the job *unless* they offered me $200,000.

4 Match the two parts to make logical sentences.

1 I'll put that in writing
2 We couldn't agree to that
3 I'd pay you all a lot more
4 We can offer you a discount

a if it was my decision.
b if you pay cash.
c if you want me to.
d unless you signed a long-term contract.

5 Which sentence implies the following?

i I can easily do something.
ii I would like to do something, but I can't.
iii We can offer you something more on one condition.
iv We can accept your request if you agree to an important condition, but we think this is unlikely.

Listening 1: Conditional offers

1 Listen to a negotiation in a small bank. The Information Technology department is being asked to change offices. What do the two sides say? Complete the sentences with the words and phrases they use. **18.1**

Conditional form using *would* or *could*	Word or phrase	Verb in the present or past tense
1 We would consider a move	_____	we get much larger offices ...
2 We'd be happy to discuss ...	_____	we can have your current offices ...
3 We would agree to move ...	_____	we got the go-ahead to hire ...
4 We could offer you ...	_____	no other department objects ...
5 We wouldn't consider ...	*unless*	you can guarantee us ...
6 I'd be willing to take ...	*if*	you agreed to move out on the 26th.

2 Listen again. Conditional offers are not always accepted; how do the two people from the IT department reject proposals unconditionally? Write the three sentences they use. **18.1**

Practice 1

A bank is negotiating with a computer supplier to buy some new workstations. Your teacher will give you a role to prepare. Use the phrases for proposals and offers from the **Language focus** above.

Work in pairs. Student A should look at **page 120**, and Student B at **page 129**.

Listening 2: Should we grant this loan?

Sally Raven, a Commercial Relationship Manager at MGS Bank, has to decide whether to lend money to a manufacturing and trading company. They want a large sum of money, so she needs to consult her superior, Chris Cook. Listen to their telephone conversation, and complete the notes below, summarizing the situation. **18.2**

Company name ....
Company manufactures ....
but can only produce ....
Company wants to sub-contract to ....
Has orders for ....
Wants to import ....
Meeting arranged for ....

Discussion

- Do you think the bank should lend money to this company for this purpose?
- What further information would be useful?
- What are the potential risks involved?
- What are the potential benefits for the bank?
- What guarantees could the bank ask for?

Practice 2

MGS Bank has arranged a meeting with Capper Trading. Your teacher will give you a role to prepare. You will need to look at your notes from **Listening 2**. In the meeting, use phrases for negotiating from the **Language focus**.

Work in pairs. Student or Group A should look at **page 120**, and Student or Group B at **page 130**.

Writing

Write a letter or an email from Sally Raven, the Commercial Relationship Manager, to the manager at Capper Trading, summarizing what has been agreed in the negotiation. Look at **Unit 4** if you need help.

19 Derivatives

AIMS

To learn about: futures, options and swaps; key vocabulary of derivatives
To learn how to: clarify, summarize and paraphrase
To practise: talking about the advantages and disadvantages of
derivatives; clarifying and summarizing key points from a talk

Lead in

- Do you know what the main types of derivatives are?
- What are the two main uses of derivatives?
- Does the organization you work for use or trade derivatives?

Reading 1: Derivatives

Read the text and do the exercises on page 90.

Traders at the Chicago Mercantile Exchange

Derivatives is a collective term for financial market products whose value depends on (i.e. is derived from) the price of another underlying asset such as a stock, a stock index (the average value of representative stocks in a given market), a currency, a commodity, etc. The main derivatives are futures, options and swaps. They were developed to allow companies to reduce uncertainty by guaranteeing future prices, at a reasonable cost. This allows companies to plan more effectively.

Futures contracts are agreements to make or take delivery of specified commodities (foodstuffs, metals, etc.) or financial instruments at a fixed future date, at a price determined when the contract is made. Futures contracts allow both sellers and buyers to hedge or reduce risks. For example, a cocoa grower can agree a price, quantity and delivery date with a chocolate manufacturer. The seller eliminates the risk that the price will drop, and the buyer the risk that it will rise. The same logic led to the development of financial futures: contracts to buy and sell stocks, stock indexes, interest rates and currencies at a future date.

Options differ from futures in that they give the right, but *not* the obligation, to buy or sell an asset at a fixed price on or before a given date. Buying a call option gives you the right to buy an asset; buying a put option gives you the right to sell an asset. For example, if you expect the price of a stock to rise you can buy the right to buy that stock in the future at the current market price. If you think the price of a stock will fall in the next few weeks or months you can buy the right to sell it in the future at the current price. If you are wrong, you do not have to exercise the option to buy or sell the stocks, but you lose the price of the option. This is the premium the writer or seller of the option receives from the buyer. Obviously, the expectations of the writer of an option about the future value of the assets are opposite to those of the buyer, and the writer does not expect the option to be exercised. Futures and options are traded by speculators hoping to make a profit from price fluctuations, as well as by companies seeking to hedge. In fact, much more derivative usage is based on speculation than hedging nowadays.

Borrowers and lenders can also swap or exchange future interest payments. A company that has borrowed money at a floating rate could protect itself from a rise in interest rates by exchanging this for a fixed interest rate loan with another company or financial institution. These are interest rate swaps. Companies can also undertake exchange rate swaps, exchanging funds in two different currencies. At a future date the same amount of the currencies is re-exchanged at a predetermined exchange rate. Over the term of the agreement, the counterparties exchange fixed or floating rate interest payments in their swapped currencies.

1 Find words and phrases in the text to complete the sentences.

1 A _____ _____ is a contract giving the possibility to sell a specified quantity of securities, foreign exchange or commodities in the future, if it is advantageous to do so.

2 _____ are raw materials such as agricultural products and metals that are traded on special exchanges.

3 _____ are forward contracts for the purchase and sale of securities, precious metals, etc., at a fixed price.

4 A _____ _____ is a contract giving the buyer the right, but not the obligation, to buy an asset in the future.

5 If you _____ you make transactions that are designed to reduce risk regarding a particular price, interest rate or exchange rate.

6 An _____ _____ _____ is an exchange of future payments on borrowed money according to specified terms.

7 If you _____ an option you use or implement the option, taking up the possibility to buy or sell something.

8 A _____ anticipates future changes in a market and makes risky transactions, hoping to make a gain.

9 A _____ is the money the writer of an option receives.

2 Use a word or phrase from each box to make word combinations from the text. You can use some words more than once. Then use some of the word combinations to complete the sentences below.

determine	interest payments
eliminate	options
exercise	prices
guarantee	risks
reduce	uncertainty
swap	

1 Companies with fixed and floating loans can choose to _____ _____ _____.

2 Futures contracts allow you to _____ short-term _____.

3 Hedging is the attempt to_____ _____; speculating is the opposite.

4 If prices move the wrong way, the buyers of _____ do not _____ them.

5 With futures, you can _____ _____ several months in advance.

Listening: Derivatives

1 Peter Sinclair, who we have already heard in other units, was formerly director of the Centre for Central Banking Studies at the Bank of England. Steve Harrison works in the compliance department of a large bank in London – you will hear him talking about regulation in **Unit 23**. Listen first to Peter Sinclair and then to Steve Harrison talking about derivatives. *19*

Who suggests that financial institutions need to take risks – Sinclair or Harrison?

2 Now listen again and answer the questions below. 🔊**19**

1 What do Sinclair and Harrison say about how long derivatives have existed?
2 What does Sinclair mean when he says derivatives 'change the structure of risks and returns'?
3 In what situation does Sinclair say a company would want to get US dollar assets ahead of time?
4 What, according to Sinclair, is the danger with derivatives?
5 What do you think Harrison means when he says derivatives 'have had a very bad press'?
6 Harrison says derivatives can be used to protect positions, but 'they can also give you exposure to areas that the bank decides that it wants to have exposure to'. What does this mean?
7 What does Harrison mean when he says 'Financial institutions are in the risk and reward business'? Do you agree?

Reading 2: An investment 'time bomb'

Read the article on derivatives and complete it using the words from the box.

clients	contracts	commodities	hedge	instruments
investment	risk	speculate	underlying	

🔴🔴🔴

NEWS

Buffett warns on investment 'time bomb'

The rapidly growing trade in derivatives poses a 'mega-catastrophic risk' for the economy, legendary investor Warren Buffett has warned. The derivatives market has exploded in recent years, with (1) _____ banks selling billions of dollars worth of these investments to (2) _____ as a way to off-load or manage market (3) _____. But Mr Buffett, the world's second-richest man, argues that such highly complex financial (4) _____ are time bombs and 'financial weapons of mass destruction' that could harm not only their buyers and sellers, but the whole economic system.

Contracts devised by 'madmen'

Derivatives are financial instruments that allow investors to (5) _____ on the future price of, for example, (6) _____ or shares – without buying the (7) _____ investment. Derivatives like futures, options and swaps were developed to allow investors to (8)_____ risks in financial markets – in effect buy insurance against market movements – but have quickly become a means of investment in their own right. Outstanding derivatives (9) _____ – excluding those traded on exchanges such as the International Petroleum Exchange – are worth close to $85 trillion, according to the International Swaps and Derivatives Association. Some derivatives contracts, Mr Buffett says, appear to have been devised by 'madmen'. In his 'Annual letter to shareholders' Mr Buffett compares the derivatives business to 'hell ... easy to enter and almost impossible to exit'.

Discussion

- Why is it possible to describe derivatives as 'weapons of mass destruction'?
- What do you think Buffett means by a 'time bomb'?
- Do you know any examples of bankruptcies resulting from derivatives trading? What happened, and why?

LANGUAGE FOCUS

Clarifying, summarizing and paraphrasing

In many business situations – such as presentations, negotiations and meetings – it is often useful to paraphrase, summarize or clarify what has been said.

1 The following sentences (1–12) contain examples from the Listening exercise. Which of the actions (a–c) could the phrases and sentences in *italics* be used for?

   a Paraphrase or clarify what someone else has said
   b Clarify or paraphrase what you have said
   c Summarize what you, or you and other people, have said

   1 *What I mean is that* some derivatives are very complicated. ☐
   2 *Can I just repeat the key information?* ☐
   3 *I'd like to run through the main points that we've talked about.* ☐
   4 *If I understand you correctly, you're saying that* derivatives can be misused. ☐
   5 *In other words,* hedging means protecting certain positions. ☐
   6 *In other words, you think* financial institutions have to take risks. ☐
   7 *Let me just go over the main points again.* ☐
   8 *So what you mean is that* derivatives aren't really new at all. ☐
   9 *Can we just summarize what we've agreed?* ☐
   10 *So what you're saying is that* banks shouldn't trade complicated derivatives. ☐
   11 *What I want to say is that* you need to adopt a balanced view. ☐
   12 *I'd like to check / confirm what we've said.* ☐

2 Working in pairs, choose a Tapescript from one of the odd-numbered units. Imagine that one of you is the speaker and the other is a listener. The listener paraphrases, summarizes or clarifies what the speaker has said, using the phrases above.

Example:
'Derivatives have had a very bad press.'
'*If I understand you correctly, you're saying that* they've had a lot of bad publicity.'

Practice

Prepare a short talk, for a company's senior management, on one of the following topics:

   1 Defending the use of derivatives
   2 Outlining the dangers of derivatives
   3 Balancing both the advantages and disadvantages of derivatives use

For examples of the dangers of derivatives, look up the bankruptcy of one or more of the following institutions on the internet: Barings Bank, Orange County, Long-Term Capital Management, WorldCom, Enron, Global Crossing.

Examples of the benefits of derivatives include the following:
   • Farmers can protect themselves from the effect of poor crop yields.
   • Manufacturers can protect themselves from fluctuating raw material prices.
   • Investors can use options to benefit from increases in stock prices but reduce their exposure to falls in price.
   • Investors (or perhaps speculators) can profit from falls in stock prices.
   • International corporations can use currency swaps to eliminate their exposure to exchange rate fluctuations.

When speaking, use some of the summarizing phrases from the **Language focus**. When listening to other learners' talks, ask questions using some of the clarifying phrases.

20 Negotiating 2

To learn how to: deal with conflict; conclude successful and unsuccessful negotiations
To practise: negotiating working conditions

Lead in

Different ways of behaving are considered normal in different parts of the world. Unfamiliarity with other people's everyday cultural practices can cause problems in international negotiations. Which of the following statements best describes normal business behaviour in your country or part of the world?

A	B
1 Decisions are made by an individual – the most senior person in a team.	1 Decisions are made by a group.
2 It is important to establish a definitive written contract that cannot be changed.	2 An agreement should only cover general principles. If a situation changes unexpectedly, an agreement can obviously be changed as well.
3 Conflict and disagreement are acceptable parts of negotiating. You don't have to be polite or diplomatic when you disagree with proposals.	3 It is important to avoid conflict and not to 'lose face' by being contradicted or losing an argument in public.
4 You can interrupt people, say 'No', threaten to end negotiations, etc.	4 It is better to say 'That's a bit difficult' or 'I'll think about it' than to say 'No'.

Discussion

- Have you ever taken part in an unsuccessful negotiation?
- What happened? Was there a cultural or behavioural problem, or were there just incompatible objectives?
- Could a successful conclusion have been reached?

Vocabulary

You are going to listen to the end of an unsuccessful negotiation. Before you listen, check your understanding of the words and phrases (1–6) below by matching them with their definitions (a–f).

1	adjourn	a	arrived at a position where no more progress is possible
2	call it a day	b	barrier or obstacle
3	give a little ground	c	compromise or make concessions
4	reached a stalemate	d	end the negotiation
5	sticking point	e	have a break in negotiations
6	where we stand	f	what our position is

Listening 1: Concluding an unsuccessful negotiation

1 Listen to the negotiation between Alice Hewlett of the National Union Bank in London and Ajay Sharma of Biztel, an Indian call centre provider, and answer the questions. **20.1**

    1 What is the sticking point?

    2 What kind of staff does the bank want to handle calls from their customers, and why do they think this may soon be impossible?

    3 What two suggestions does Ajay Sharma make, and how does Alice Hewlett respond?

2 Write the phrases that are used to do the following things:

1 Ask why the other side does not agree:
2 Suggest finding a compromise:
3 Ask the other side to suggest a compromise solution:
4 Suggest having a break in negotiations:
5 Say they will need to find another business partner:

3 Can you think of any other phrases to do these things? Add them to the table above.

Dealing with conflict

When a negotiation seems to have reached a stalemate, you can:

a End the negotiation
b Temporarily postpone talking about the sticking point
c Try to find a compromise solution

Which of these actions (a–c) could the following phrases and sentences be used for?

1 As this seems to be getting in the way of an agreement, maybe we should look at the next point? ☐
2 Can we look at this in a bit more detail? What exactly is your objection to … ☐
3 I really don't think we're going to reach agreement on this. ☐
4 I think it would be a good idea to come back to this later. ☐
5 I think we both need to reconsider our positions. Meanwhile, can we … ☐
6 I think we've gone as far as we can today. ☐
7 Let us just explain our position. ☐
8 Perhaps we can set this point aside until later, and move on to another issue? ☐
9 Well, one way out of this would be if you … ☐

Discussion

Think of all the negotiations you have taken part in, both in your business life and in your personal life. Which was the most successful? Why do you think it succeeded?

Listening 2: Concluding a successful negotiation

Listen to the end of a successful negotiation between a computer manufacturer and a large bank. This is the negotiation from Unit 18, Practice 1. 🔘 20.2

1 **In what order does the speaker do the following things?**

   a Expresses satisfaction at the result of the negotiation
   b Finishes negotiating the last item by accepting a proposal
   c Looks ahead to future deals
   d Proposes to draw up a contract
   e Summarizes the negotiation

2 **Now listen again and write the phrases the speaker uses to do these things. 🔘 20.2**

3 **Can you think of any other phrases that you could use?**

"Any other objections?"

Useful phrases

Phrases for offering to confirm something in writing include:

We'll put together a written proposal.
We'll write a contract tomorrow.

Phrases to show satisfaction and look ahead to future deals include:

That seems to be a very good arrangement.
We look forward to a successful partnership.
I look forward to our next meeting.

Listening 3: Saturday opening

Listen to two employees of MGS Bank discussing a planned extension of opening hours, and answer the questions below. **⊘ 20.3**

1 What changes are MGS Bank planning to make to opening hours?
2 How are they planning to compensate staff for these changes?
3 Why is it uncertain whether the staff will get more money?

Business News

MGS announces Saturday opening

In line with a growing trend, MGS Bank has announced that, starting early next year, most of its branches will be open on Saturdays. The exact hours have yet to be decided. Robin Black, Head of Customer Services at MGS, said yesterday, 'Hole-in-the-wall banking and the internet have made banking more convenient. But there's still a need for face-to-face banking, at a time when it's convenient to customers. It's virtually impossible for many people to get away from work or home during the week to make a deposit or bank a cheque. Our Saturday opening will also be of great benefit to small businesses operating at weekends.'

More and more banks are opening on Saturdays.

Practice

The day after the conversation you heard in **Listening 3**, MGS Bank informed all their staff of their plans for extended opening hours, and the article above appeared in a newspaper.

Unsurprisingly, the bank's staff association is not very keen on Saturday opening. A meeting to negotiate new working conditions has been arranged. Your teacher will give you a role to prepare. In the negotiation, use phrases from the **Language focus** and the **Useful phrases** in this unit. You may also want to look back at **Unit 18**.

Work in pairs. Student or Team A should look at **page 120**, and Student or Team B at **page 129**.

21 Asset management

AIMS

To learn about: asset and fund management; key vocabulary of asset
management and allocation

To learn how to: disagree diplomatically

To practise: talking to a client about their investment portfolio

Lead in

- If you had a large amount of money to invest, would you invest it yourself, or get a professional investment consultant to do it?
- Would you like to invest and manage other people's money?
- What are the different basic strategies of asset management?

Listening 1: Asset management and allocation

1   Paula Foley is an investment consultant in New York. Listen to her talking about asset management. Which three of the following things does she <u>not</u> mention? **21.1**

allocation	diversification	liabilities	portfolios	size
derivatives	interest	objectives	risk	style

2   Read the statements below, which summarize what Paula Foley says, and then listen again. In what order does she say these things? **21.1**

a   Asset allocation means deciding how much to invest in different classes of investments: bonds, stocks and so on. ☐

b   Asset management involves investing in bonds, stocks, cash, precious metals and funds. ☐

c   How you manage assets depends on the client's objectives and the portfolio's size. ☐

d   If you diversify too much it becomes too expensive. ☐

e   It's easier to diversify a large portfolio than a small one. ☐

f   Objectives can be either long term or short term. ☐

g   The risk of a portfolio depends largely on the expected returns. ☐

Listening 2: Investment styles

1   Listen to Paula Foley talking about investment styles. How many styles does she mention? **21.2**

2 Now listen again and complete the notes below. **21.2**

Growth investment means looking for _____

Value investment is investing in _____

Large companies are generally _____

Small companies often _____

Active management means you _____

Passive investment means you _____

Index-linked portfolios try to _____

Even fund portfolios need _____

3 Use a word from each box to make common word combinations. One word can be used twice.

asset	accumulation
capital	earnings
conservative	industries
growth	investment
investment	management
stable	values

Reading: Fund management

The article opposite, from *The Economist*, was published in 2002 after actively managed equity funds in Britain had lost over 30% (on average) in 30 months. This was only 1% less than passive, index-linked funds. Read the article, and answer the questions below it.

mug = a person who doesn't know very much and is easy to take advantage of

come into their own = be successful

futile (adjective) = unsuccessful, a waste of time

handsomely rewarded = well paid

trigger (verb) = cause, provoke

upfront = paid in advance

better off = richer, or in a better situation

slim (adjective) = small

Fund management: Mug's game

Anger is growing with those who manage money, particularly with those poorly performing active managers who claimed that it was precisely during tough times that they would come into their own against indexed funds. In Britain, two-thirds of active managers underperformed the index last year, even before the fees that they charged are subtracted. Those people are handsomely rewarded for losing money. Each year they pocket 1–2% of the assets they manage, on top of initial charges of as much as 5%. Indexers, by contrast, charge only 0.5% a year, with no upfront fees.

An average fund manager will beat the market some of the time. Over the long run, though, the great majority of fund managers will do no better than the market average, particularly once their charges are taken into account. The chances are slim of finding one of those blessed few who can show real, sustained skill in stock-picking. Even if you find one, you may discover that what made him good in one economic period will serve him less well in the next.

Believers in the so-called efficient-market hypothesis, developed by American economists in the 1960s, have tried to demonstrate the impossibility of consistent outperformance. They argue that all useful information that is available to market participants is already factored into a company's share price. Additional analysis of a share by, for instance, taking a closer look at a company's books or talking to its management – as well as all attempts at discovering patterns in price movements – will be futile. This theory opened the door to those offering merely to track the index. Index-tracking grew hugely during the bull market of the 1980s and 1990s. In the bear market of the past two years, people have not pulled out much money from index funds – or at least, not yet.

Not everybody buys the efficient-market hypothesis, however. George Soros, a well-known speculator, thinks he made his money because markets often over- or undervalue things. He also challenges the view that share prices are simply a passive reflection of underlying value, or of the expected earnings of a company. A high share price might, for example, trigger certain actions: a public offering of a company's shares, or a merger or an acquisition. A low share price, meanwhile, might stop plans for an initial public offering or a merger. This is what Soros calls the market's 'reflexivity'.

If knowledge of such a two-way relationship between share prices and assets can be put to good use, a fund manager might consistently do better than the market. Peter Lynch, formerly of Fidelity Investments, showed that a more old-fashioned technique – looking for good companies that the market fails for a time to appreciate – can also outperform. Yet a few examples among a cast of many thousands of fund managers offer only small consolation to the average investor, who will almost always be better off – or these days, rather worse off – putting his money in an index fund.

1 Why are people getting angry with active money managers?
2 Why did indexed funds develop?
3 What is the efficient-market hypothesis? Why does it suggest that it is impossible to beat the market?
4 What is George Soros's argument against the efficient-market hypothesis?
5 How did Peter Lynch beat the market?
6 Why does the article recommend that the average investor should use a passive index-linked fund rather than an actively managed one?

Discussion

Do you agree with the people who say that it is impossible to beat the stock market, on average?

LANGUAGE FOCUS

Using diplomatic language

People working in finance occasionally need to disagree with customers, and politely suggest or explain to them that they are wrong or mistaken. This is often done in a diplomatic and indirect way. Can you think of any phrases to do this, or can you remember any from **Unit 12**?

Match the direct statements (1–6) with the more diplomatic phrases (a–f).

1 That's a bad idea!
2 I completely disagree with you!
3 You can't just transfer all your funds!
4 That's illogical!
5 That'll make things worse!
6 You shouldn't do that!

a I'm not entirely sure about that.
b I'm not sure that that would make things any better.
c I'm afraid I don't think that's very logical.
d Don't you think it would / might be a good idea to ...?
e Perhaps you should consider a different investment strategy?
f Maybe it would be better to just transfer some of your funds?

Practice

An investment advisor has a meeting with a client. They have very different ideas as to how the client's money should be invested. Your teacher will give you a role to prepare. The investment advisor should use the diplomatic language from the **Language focus** above. Both sides may need to use the phrases for making, accepting and rejecting proposals in **Unit 18**.

Work in pairs. Student A should look at **page 121**, and Student B at **page 131**.

Writing

After the **Practice** meeting, you need to write a letter or an email to summarize what happened.

1 If you were the investment advisor in the role play:

Write an email to the client proposing the changes you want to make to his / her portfolio, and asking him / her to confirm that he / she accepts them. Then write an email to your boss explaining the situation – what the client wants to do, what you have suggested, and why – as you think the client might complain.

2 If you were the client in the role play:

Write a letter to the Wealth Management Director of the bank, complaining that the person responsible for your account does not seem to know enough about asset management and does not listen to you, and that you want someone more senior to take over responsibility for your account.

22 Presentations 1

To learn about: presenting skills, learning styles
To learn how to: structure a presentation; introduce a presentation; prepare visual aids
To practise: writing and giving the first part of a presentation

Lead in

- Do you have to make presentations?
- Are they generally formal, or informal?
- Who do you present to – colleagues, superiors, current or potential clients, investors? How does this affect what you say?

Discussion

- What makes a good presenter?
- What makes a good presentation?

"Life is just one big presentation for you, isn't it?"

Reading: Learning styles

1   In any presentation, it's important to think about your audience and how they are going to understand your message. Different people have different learning styles, which affect how they respond to presentations. Do you know what your learning style is? Look at the statements in the boxes (1–3) below and decide which box contains the most statements that are true for you.

1
- [ ] I learn by watching.
- [ ] I remember things I have seen.
- [ ] I remember things by picturing them in my mind.
- [ ] I find it easy to remember people's faces.
- [ ] I find graphs, charts and diagrams very useful.
- [ ] I need to write things down to remember them.
- [ ] I prefer written directions or instructions to spoken ones.
- [ ] I usually take notes during lessons, talks and presentations.
- [ ] I often highlight or underline texts while reading them.

2

- ☐ I learn by listening.
- ☐ I remember things I have heard.
- ☐ I like taking part in discussions.
- ☐ I find it easy to remember voices and music.
- ☐ I'm good at remembering the words to songs.
- ☐ I prefer listening to a good lecture to reading about the same material.
- ☐ I prefer spoken directions or instructions to written ones.
- ☐ I don't usually take notes during lessons, talks and presentations.
- ☐ I sometimes talk to myself or think out loud.

3

- ☐ I learn by doing.
- ☐ I remember things I have done.
- ☐ I don't like sitting still for a long time and need regular physical activity.
- ☐ I make a lot of gestures and movements while talking.
- ☐ I often stand close to people and touch them while talking to them.
- ☐ I think and solve problems and get ideas while doing physical activity.
- ☐ I quickly notice if a chair is uncomfortable.
- ☐ I often play with keys, coins, pens or other small objects in my hand.
- ☐ I like working with tools.

2 Now match the boxes (1–3) to the statements about learning styles (a–c) below.

a People with a mainly *kinaesthetic* learning style are at a disadvantage when they have to sit still during a presentation.

b If people in your audience have a mainly *visual* learning style, you can help them by using visual aids in your presentation.

c Those with a mainly *auditory* learning style are usually at an advantage when learning through a presentation.

Visual aids

1 Read the two slides giving information about effective use of visual aids.

> **Slides should be:**
>
> - **ready** (there should not be a long pause while you look for them, or turn on the equipment)
>
> - **large and clear, not too detailed, and visible to the whole of your audience**
>
> - **displayed for long enough for the audience to read them** (you should not use more than one a minute)
>
> - laid out clearly, in **bullet points** rather than long sentences or paragraphs.

You should check the equipment before starting. For example:

- Does the projector work?

- Can you connect your laptop to the projector?

- Can everyone see you and the screen, or do you need to move the chairs?

- Is their any light reflecting on the screen – do you need to close the blinds or dim the lights?

2 Now rewrite the following paragraphs as slides, each containing five bulleted pieces of information.

1 A good introduction usually contains a welcome to the audience, and thanks them for coming. It states the subject or title of the presentation and its purpose. It outlines the structure of the presentation, often by giving a list of the main points to be covered. It will usually state how long the presentation will take, and tell the audience when the speaker would like them to ask questions: at any time, or at the end.

2 The end of a presentation should include a clear signal that the speaker has finished or is about to finish the last point, so that anyone who has lost concentration will realise that the main part is almost over. The speaker can then repeat the main points of the presentation a final time, and draw some logical conclusions. This means that speakers often make their most important points three times: in the introduction, they say that they are going to say something; in the middle part, they say it; and at the end, they say that they have said it. The ending generally includes thanks for listening, and an invitation to ask questions.

3 Visual aids can also contain charts, graphs and diagrams. Do you know the names for the different types (a–c) shown below?

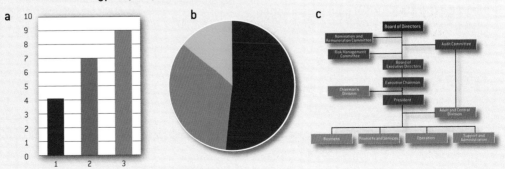

Useful phrases

1 Complete the phrases for the introduction of a presentation using the correct form of the words from the box.

draw	go	hesitate	see
feel	have	save	take

a If there's anything you don't understand, please don't _____ to interrupt.

b I'd like to _____ your attention to ...

c I'm _____ to talk for about 15 minutes.

d I'd appreciate it if you would _____ any questions until the end.

e As you can _____ from this slide ...

f My presentation will _____ about 20 minutes.

g I'd like you to _____ a look at this ...

h Please _____ free to ask questions at any time.

2 Now put the phrases into the table below. You will add more phrases later.

1 Greet the audience:	
2 Introduce yourself:	
3 Give the title or subject of your presentation:	
4 Tell the audience the length of your presentation:	
5 Describe the structure of your presentation:	
6 Refer to visual aids:	
7 Tell the audience they can interrupt:	
8 Request that the audience asks questions at the end:	

Listening: The introduction

1 You are going to listen to an introduction to a presentation about conservative portfolio strategies. Before you listen, think of phrases that could be used for the following things:

   1 Greeting the audience
   2 Introducing yourself
   3 Giving the title or subject of your presentation
   4 Describing the structure of your presentation

2 Now listen to the introduction and answer the questions below. **⊘22**

   1 Which things from the list (1–4) above does the speaker do?
   2 What phrases does she use to do them? Add them to the **Useful phrases** table opposite.
   3 Does she use any other phrases that can be added to the table?

3 Listen again, and complete the slide that the speaker shows while describing the structure of her presentation. **⊘22**

Conservative portfolio strategies

-
-
-
-

Practice

You are going to prepare an introduction to a short presentation. Your teacher will help you to choose a subject from **page 136**. Use some of the phrases from the **Useful phrases** and **Listening** to link your ideas together.

The full presentation will contain three or four parts, so your introduction should mention this. Do not write everything you are going to say – only make a few notes. Remember that the aim of the activity is to practise the phrases – the actual content is less important at this stage. Do <u>not</u> prepare a whole presentation.

Remember: it is not only what you say that is important, but also how you say it – your presentation style. You should appear relaxed, positive and confident.

23 Regulating the financial sector

To learn about: financial regulation, managing conflicts of interest
To learn how to: use suffixes and prefixes
To practise: talking about conflicts of interest and ethical choices

Lead in

- Why are financial institutions supervised and regulated? If they were not regulated, what could they do that would not be in their customers' best interests?
- Have you ever had any problems as a customer with the products or services of a financial institution?

Reading: Conflicts of interest

Conflicts of interest are situations in which what is good for one department of a financial institution and its customers is not in the best interests of another department and its customers. Such conflicts are almost inevitable in financial institutions.

Read the four paragraphs below. In each case:

1 What is the potential problem arising from this situation?

2 What is done (or what could or should be done) to prevent the problem arising?

    a Banks that underwrite security issues (shares, bonds, etc.) for companies are obliged to buy the securities if they are unable to sell them to other financial institutions or to the public.

    b Analysts in the research departments of large banks study the financial situation of companies, and write reports about them for potential investors. In doing so, the analysts learn a great deal about companies, and so are often in a position to give them advice about raising capital, etc. However, they are usually competing with other banks to get business from these companies.

    c Auditors know a lot about accounting methods and acquire a lot of information about the companies whose accounts they audit. This puts them in a very good position to obtain extra – and generally very lucrative – consulting work with these companies.

    d People working in banks' corporate finance and mergers and acquisitions departments often have information about takeover bids and other deals that are being planned but have not yet been announced.

Vocabulary 1

You are going to listen to Steve Harrison, who works in the compliance department of a large bank in London, talking about financial regulation. Before you listen, check your understanding of the words and phrases in the box by matching them with their definitions (1–6).

compliance	mandate	supervision
counterparties	statutory	wholesale

1 according to a law or regulation
2 authorization given to an organization to carry out specific responsibilities
3 following rules and regulations
4 working with companies and institutions, and not personal or retail customers
5 other institutions in an agreement, contract or transaction
6 watching over people or an organization to make sure they are behaving correctly

Listening 1: The Financial Services Authority

1 Steve Harrison is in regular contact with the relationship management team at the FSA that is responsible for supervising his bank. Listen to an interview with him. Which of the following points does he mention? **23.1**

   1 The formation of the FSA
   2 How banks are changing
   3 The companies that are part of the FSA
   4 The objectives of the FSA
   5 Regulating consumers

2 Now listen again and answer the questions below. **23.1**

   1 Why was the FSA created?
   2 Which of the FSA's statutory objectives does Harrison mention?
   3 What does the FSA want to understand when working with institutions?
   4 What are a bank's 'wholesale counterparties'?

Listening 2: Conflicts of interest

1 Listen to Steve Harrison talking about conflicts of interest. According to what he says, are the following statements true or false? **23.2**

   1 Conflicts of interest in financial institutions can be avoided.
   2 The problem generally involves access to information.
   3 Financial institutions bought shares falsely recommended by research analysts.
   4 Analysts recommended investing in firms in the hope that these firms would give them investment banking work.
   5 The number of recommendations to sell shares is probably too high.
   6 It is legitimate for an auditing firm to do extra consultancy work.
   7 Many auditing firms have been forced by law to split off their consultancy business from the auditing firm.
   8 Many companies now use different auditing firms for auditing and consultancy work.

2 What are the two examples Steve Harrison gives of conflicts of interest? Did you mention these in the earlier **Reading** activity?

3 Are there any conflicts of interest that occur in the organization you work for? How are they dealt with?

Word formation

Steve Harrison talks about *regulation* and the *regulator*. The FSA (a *regulatory* authority) *regulates* financial services in the UK. So despite a certain amount of *deregulation*, the financial industry is still *regulated* (as opposed to *unregulated*).

There are lots of word groups like this in English. Verbs can be made into nouns and vice versa, and nouns can be made into adjectives and adverbs, by adding suffixes. Examples:

Verbs	Nouns	Adjectives	Adverbs
analyze/analyse	analysis analyst	analytic analytical	analytically
capitalize	capital capitalist	capitalist	

Complete the table below, then mark the stressed syllable in each word. Some boxes will contain several words. You heard some of these words in the **Listening** activities; you will need to use some in the **Discussion** opposite. Use a dictionary to check your answers.

Verbs	Concrete and abstract nouns	Nouns for people or organizations	Adjectives	Negative adjectives
account (for)	accounting			
advise				
		consultant		
deal (with)				
			industrial	
	investment			
				unmanageable
			organized	
	profit			
	value			

Common suffixes include: *-ing, -ment, -ation, -ness, -ility* (to make nouns)
                                     -er, -or, -ist (to make nouns for people or occupations)
                                       -ize, -ise (to make verbs)
                                       -able, -ed (to make adjectives)

Prefixes for negatives include: *un-, dis-, non-*

Vocabulary 2

Complete the sentences below, using the correct forms of the words in brackets. Look at the table in the **Language focus** to help you.

1   The (consult) _____ believed that the company needed stricter financial (manage) _____ and suggested withdrawing (profit) _____ product lines.
2   The newly (industry) _____ countries still need a lot of (invest) _____.
3   The investigators talked to the chief (account) _____ who gave them some (value) _____ information.
4   It would be (advice) _____ to (consult) _____ a lawyer before talking to the investigators.
5   The raiders thought the large company had become (manage) _____. The managers accused the raiders of being (profit) _____.
6   A company's (manage) _____ are (account) _____ to the shareholders.
7   In (account) _____ , there are various ways of (value) _____ assets.
8   For years I thought my investment (advice) _____ was absolutely (value) _____. But then he told me to buy some dot.com stocks which soon became totally (value) _____.

Discussion

The situations described below involve well-known conflicts of interest and require people to make ethical choices. What would you do in these situations, and why? Discuss them in pairs or groups. Use some of the words from the **Vocabulary** exercise above in your discussion.

1   You get a job in a bank's mergers and acquisitions department. One of your new colleagues informs you, 'Whenever we know that Company A is going to take over Company B, and that Company B's stocks are going to rise, we go out and buy some of Company B's stocks. We make a profit, but nobody loses, because the stocks we buy had already been sold by somebody else. OK, this is called "insider dealing", but what's the problem? It shouldn't be a crime.'

? What will you do about this?

2   You are an economic advisor to a minister in a new government that has just been elected in a country where the central bank is independent. Several members of the government want to take back control of interest rate policy. After all, the government has been elected; the central bankers have not. If the government controlled interest rate decisions it could keep rates low in the months before the next election. Consequently many voters would be paying less on their mortgages and other debts, and have more money to spend.

    ? What would you recommend?

3   You work in the research department of a bank. You have written a report which demonstrates that a local manufacturing company would be a good takeover target for the market leader in the industry. This multinational company could modernize the local company's factory and produce goods more efficiently. But it would probably also take over all the company's other functions, and close down the local marketing, sales, research and development, finance, and human resources departments, resulting in a lot of people losing their jobs. Another possibility would even be for the new owners to close down everything, and move production elsewhere. This would have a catastrophic effect on your town.

    ? Will you still submit a report recommending a takeover?

4   You are a shareholder in a local manufacturing company. A group of shareholders wants to force the company to show more corporate social responsibility. They have proposed a motion for the Annual General Meeting, stating 'Before making decisions, this company will consider their impact on all the company's stakeholders – staff, customers, suppliers and the local community – as well as on the environment in general.' Other shareholders oppose the motion, arguing that a company's principal purpose is to maximize returns to its shareholders.

    ? How will you vote at the AGM?

"Let me get back to you on that—I've got an office full of people right now."

24 Presentations 2

AIMS

To learn about: the parts of a presentation
To learn how to: end a presentation; deal with questions
To practise: making a complete presentation

Lead in

- How long do you think you can concentrate totally on what someone else is saying, without thinking about anything else?
- What is the ideal length of time for a presentation?

Discussion

Which of the following comments about presentations do you agree with?

1 'Beginnings and endings of presentations are often very similar.'

6 'It's important to link the different parts of your presentation, with standard phrases.'

2 'The central part or main body of the presentation is the most difficult to prepare.'

3 'No one in the audience concentrates all the time during a presentation.'

4 'Dealing with questions is one of the easiest parts of the presentation.'

5 'In many presentations, the main points are repeated three times.'

Listening 1: Parts of a presentation

1 Listen to the following extracts from a presentation about financial derivatives, and complete the phrases used to signal the beginning and end of the different parts. **24.1**

OK, so as I said, (1) _____ _____ _____ _____ _____ _____ _____ _____ financial futures, (2) _____ _____ _____ _____ options ...

(5) _____ _____ _____ _____ _____ _____ _____ options, so (6) _____ _____ _____ _____ _____ _____ _____ the third part of my presentation, which is about swaps.

(3) _____ _____ _____ _____ _____ _____ _____ futures, so that completes the first part of my talk. (4) _____ _____ _____ _____ options ...

So that was interest rate swaps. (7) _____ _____ _____ _____ exchange rate swaps, which ...

2 Listen again to check your answers. **24.1**

Practice 1

Use some of the phrases from **Listening 1** to introduce and end four parts of a presentation, on the subject you chose in **Unit 22**. Decide what the topics of the different parts are, and practise sentences to begin and end them.

Listening 2: The end of a presentation

1 You are going to listen to Paula Foley, who you heard in **Unit 22**, concluding her presentation about conservative portfolio strategies. Before you listen, match the stages of the end of a presentation with the phrases from Paula's presentation.

1 Begin to summarize the main information
2 Draw some logical conclusions from what has been said
3 Thank your audience
4 Invite your audience to ask questions

a OK, that's all I have to say about capital preservation and accumulation, so now I'll just summarize my three main points again.
b Does anyone have any questions or comments?
c So, to conclude, I have two recommendations.
d Thank you all for your attention.

2 Now listen to the end of the presentation. What are Paula's two recommendations? **24.2**

Useful phrases

Here are some more phrases for ending presentations:

So, to sum up ...
I'll end by emphasizing the main points.

Thank you for your time.
Thanks for listening.

... and now I'd like to invite your questions.
Now I'd be interested to hear your comments.
Now we have twenty minutes for discussion.

Practice 2

Prepare an ending to the presentation you started in **Unit 22**. Your ending should include a summary, a conclusion, and an invitation to the audience to respond. Use the phrases from **Listening 2** and the **Useful phrases** above.

Dealing with questions and troubleshooting

Dealing with questions

The question and answer section can be the most difficult part of a presentation because you can't prepare for it.

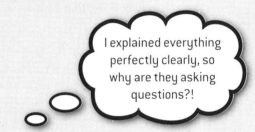

I explained everything perfectly clearly, so why are they asking questions?!

Here are some tips:

- Welcome questions and listen carefully (and look at the questioner).
- Do not interrupt the speaker.
- Clarify the exact meaning of the question if you are not sure.

Examples:

Sorry, I didn't catch that. Could you repeat that please?
Sorry, I'm not sure if I've understood exactly ...
If I've understood you correctly, you want to know ... Is that right?

- Take time to think (though not too long) before you answer, if necessary.
- Be as brief and direct as possible.
- Be polite.
- Check that your questioner is satisfied with your answer.

Examples:

Have I answered your question?
Does that answer your question?

1   Sometimes, it is impossible to answer a question, because:

   a   It is not relevant to your presentation
   b   You simply don't know the answer
   c   You don't want to give the information

In which of the situations above could you use these answers?

1   I'm afraid I don't have that information with me.
2   I'm afraid I'm not in a position to comment on that.
3   I'm afraid that doesn't really relate to my presentation. Perhaps you could discuss that with Mr X.
4   That's a difficult question to answer in a few words. Could we talk about it later?
5   Can I check on that and get back to you?

Troubleshooting

2   In presentations, it's important to be prepared for the unexpected, but it's impossible to predict every situation. Decide what you would say in the following situations. As well as phrases from this unit, you could also use some of the language from **Unit 10** (Chairing a meeting), **Unit 11** (Checking and confirming), **Unit 19** (Clarifying), **Unit 20** (Dealing with conflict) and **Unit 21** (Diplomacy).

1   You want to start, but everyone is talking.
2   Somebody at the back can't hear you.
3   You try to use the projector, but nothing happens.
4   Somebody can't understand what you're saying.
5   Somebody asks you a question on a very sensitive subject.
6   You have a mental block and can't remember the next thing you planned to say.
7   Somebody asks you a question but you don't understand what they say.
8   Somebody interrupts your presentation (although in the introduction, you asked for questions at the end).
9   Somebody interrupts you and starts talking about a completely different topic.

Practice 3

Prepare a 10–15 minute presentation on the topic you chose in **Unit 22**. Your presentation should follow the form outlined there and in this unit. Pay attention to the structure of your talk, the introduction, the different parts of the information you present, the summary and conclusion. Prepare slides to accompany your presentation.

"And that, as you can see, explains nothing."

File cards

Unit 1 Role A
Call 1: The bank

You work at a bank's call centre, answering customer enquiries. A customer calls asking for more information about the 'e-saver' account. Use the information below to answer the customer's questions.

	e-saver	Regular saver
Minimum deposit to open account	£1	
Telephone / internet banking	✓	
Overdraft facility	✗	
Instant access to funds	✓	
Higher interest rate for higher balances	✗	
Minimum deposit each month	No minimum	
Monthly statements	✗	
Arrange transactions (e.g. bill payments) online	✓	
ATM card	✗	

Call 2: The customer

Now you are a customer interested in opening a 'regular saver' account, and you want to know about the terms and conditions. Call the bank and ask questions to find out more information, and complete the table above.

Unit 2, Practice 1 Role A: Kim Brown, Assistant to the Risk Manager

You are the Assistant to Jean Chance, the Risk Manager of a large bank. You are taking part in a conference call with Robin Black in Retail Banking, Pat Green in Corporate Banking and Chris White in Mergers & Acquisitions. You need them all to attend an urgent meeting with your boss, between 8.30 and 9.30 tomorrow morning.

Greet your colleagues. Explain why you are calling.

Do not take 'no' for an answer. Insist that they rearrange any other appointments if necessary.

Unit 2, Practice 2 Role A: Student

Call a company for information about their International Graduate Training Programme.
You want to know:
- what qualifications you need
- how long the training takes
- how much you would be paid
- where the training would take place
- how to apply.

Unit 3 Role A: Chief Operating Officer

You have called this meeting and you will chair the meeting. You know that the Head of Retail Operations and the Head of Internet Banking have very different views on this matter. You will ask your two colleagues to present their arguments and to explain what they think will happen in the future. You can ask for any further information you consider necessary, and then decide what course of action to recommend to the Board of Directors next week. To prepare for the meeting, try to imagine what your two colleagues will say, and what information you will have to ask for if it isn't presented.

Unit 4 Role A: Researcher 1

Your department is doing some internet research on mortgages. Call your colleague, and tell them that the following web addresses might be useful. You will need to spell out the addresses.

http://www.bankrate.com/brm/rate/mtg_home.asp

http://www.law.cornell.edu/wex/index.php/Mortgage

Give your colleague the following email address too:

info@homeloans.mgs-bank.com

Then write down the addresses your colleague gives you.

Unit 5, Practice 1 Role A: Bank team member

You are part of a team on the bank's training course. Look at the summaries of two loan applications below; summarize them to the other team members and listen to their summaries. Then discuss all the applications in your team, and make a preliminary recommendation in each case: do you think the bank should make the loan or not? Remember that riskier loans can be more profitable for the bank, but after a certain point, the risk of default or non-payment becomes too great.

Finally, put the loans you think the bank should grant in order of priority.

Case 1	Decision: Yes / No	Priority: ____
A start-up company manufacturing computer components is having unexpected success. Its factory is operating 16 hours a day and the company is producing and selling twice as much as expected. But it has to pay its suppliers after 30 days, and its customers only pay after 60 days, so it has an enormous cash flow problem. The credit line the company has arranged is inadequate. It wants to borrow $400,000 immediately, and expects to be able to pay back within a year.		

Case 6	Decision: Yes / No	Priority: ____
A film production company that has not made a profitable film for three years needs to borrow $2 million to complete a movie currently in production. Without this money the film will have to be abandoned and $8 million will be lost. The film features two actors who have made a lot of successful films in the past. The loan would be repaid in nine months' time when the film is released, if it is successful.		

Unit 5, Practice 2 Role A: Bank customer advisor
Meeting 1

You have been having a meeting with one of the customers in Case 2 of **Practice 1** (see below) and you have just granted the loan. Before you end the meeting, you want to advise the customer to transfer all their accounts to your bank, and recommend that they use appropriate products and services from your bank. Use the information in the web page below.

Case 2	**Decision**: Yes

Two garage mechanics want to set up their own small car repair business. They are confident that they will have enough customers. They both have 20 years' experience as car mechanics, working for somebody else, but no experience of running a business. But as they point out, nobody has this experience until they run their first business! They want to borrow $50,000, paying back $10,000 a year for five years.

www.metropolis-bank.com/business/services

Search

Our Business Bank Account
Our Business Services
Business banking made easy
Business Overdraft
Business mortgages
Business Insurance
Understanding your business
Business Advice & Tips
Business News
Your Personal Finance

Our Services for Business Customers

Business Checking Account: Pay no monthly service fee for 12 months.

Business Money Market Account: Get great rates to make your money work harder.

Business Online: Monitor and manage your cash flow. View balances, transactions and funds availability on your account; view cleared checks and deposit slips; print statements; transfer funds between your accounts; make payments at home and abroad at your convenience; send checks overnight.

Business Banking Card: To pay for everyday business expenses, make deposits, check balances and transfer funds between accounts.

Merchant Credit Card Account: Enables merchants to accept credit cards from customers.

Safe Deposit Boxes: Make sure your valuables are securely tucked away in an affordable Safe Deposit box.

TaxDirect: Pay your taxes electronically with our secure service. We offer a fast, safe and convenient way to pay federal, state and local taxes.

Lines of Credit: To help you meet short-term funding needs, such as increasing inventory, dealing with seasonal cash flows or taking advantage of unplanned opportunities.

Fixed-term Loans: For when your business is ready for expansion, and needs equipment, vehicles or other fixed assets. The assets you purchase can usually secure the loan.

Executive Life Insurance: To enable your business to make the transition from one generation of top management to the next. Our Executive Life Insurance plan will ensure business continuity and also reduce taxes.

Unit 5, Practice 2 Role A: Customer

Meeting 2

You are one of the customers in Case 5 of **Practice 1** (see below) and you have been having a meeting with the bank advisor, who has just granted your loan. Before you end the meeting, the bank advisor wants to talk to you about other accounts and services the bank can offer. Listen and ask questions.

Case 5	Decision: Yes
Two hotel school graduates who have specialized in restaurant management want to borrow $20,000 to pay the franchise fee to open a new branch of a well-known, profitable and expanding international fast food chain. They expect to be able to repay the loan within two years.	

Unit 8, Practice 1 Role A

Meeting 1: Host

You are Chris Black. A business partner you have not met before, Pat Brown, is waiting for you at the reception desk of your company. Greet the visitor, introduce yourself, and make small talk.

Meeting 2: Visitor

You are Robin White. You are visiting a company and have just finished a first meeting with your host, Kim Green, and you are now having coffee together. Answer your host's questions, and/or ask questions yourself, about where your host lives, where they come from originally, their family, their hobbies, etc.

If you are invited to dinner this evening, choose whether to accept or decline.

Unit 8, Practice 3 Role A: Visitor

You have been having lunch with people from another company after a meeting, but now you have to leave. You need to make sure they have your contact details as you want to meet again next month when they come to Paris. Thank them for arranging your transport to the airport.

Unit 10 Student A

You are the training manager. You are chairing the meeting. You have to open it, explain its purpose, decide who speaks, bring people into the discussion, stop people talking too much or interrupting or digressing, etc.

Unit 11 Role A: Customer

You work for Capper Trading. You have a couple of export orders coming up, but you are not sure exactly how you want to arrange transport, insurance, customs documentation and so on. The bank's website gives details about Incoterms. You phone the bank for further information about the following things.

You don't understand:

- the difference between FAS (Free Alongside Ship) and FOB (Free On Board).
- the difference between DES (Delivered Ex Ship) and DEQ (Delivered Ex Quay).
- under which circumstances the seller is responsible for arranging and paying for insurance against damage to the goods during transportation.
- whether DDU (Delivered Duty Unpaid) and DDP (Delivered Duty Paid) apply inthe European Union.

Unit 12, Practice 1 Student A

You have the following opinions. Take turns – express one of the opinions to your partner, ask what his / her opinions are on the topic, and agree or disagree. Then listen to one of your partner's opinions, and agree or disagree.

- Commercial banks are often really incompetent.
- English is very easy to spell and pronounce.
- It's really difficult to raise the capital to start a new company.
- Men almost never admit that they're wrong.
- Most auditing companies don't do their job very well.
- People are motivated mainly by money.
- Taxes are too high in this country.
- Twenty-five years old is much too young to get married.

Unit 12, Practice 2 Role A: Chief Executive

You are having a meeting with the Human Resources Director, the Head of Customer Services, the Public Relations Director and the Finance Director. You will chair the meeting. You decide who should speak, and in which order. Control the meeting firmly, preventing interruptions or people speaking without permission.

You can start by giving your opinion if you want to, or you can wait until you have heard your colleagues speak. Personally you are in favour of outsourcing your telephone banking operation to India, as the lower salaries for 50 call centre staff will constitute a significant saving. But you could still be persuaded to change your mind if your colleagues have good arguments.

Decision-making meetings should reach decisions, so make sure that this meeting ends with a firm decision – no compromise is possible.

Unit 15, Practice 1 Student A

Describe the changes in the share prices of Citibank to your partner using the graph below. Do not let your partner see your graph.

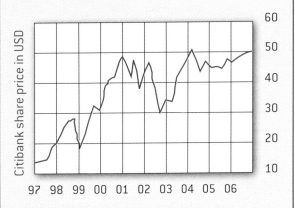

Now draw the graph that your partner describes to you.

Unit 17, Practice 2 Role A: Chief Executive

In this meeting you have to decide what to recommend to the shareholders: accept the bid, wait for a better one, or try to remain independent. At the end of the meeting, you will need to make a decision which will then be passed on to the Board.

You will chair the meeting. You should begin by asking everyone to introduce themselves. Then you can decide who should speak, and in which order. You can begin by giving your opinion if you want to, or you can wait until you have heard your colleagues speak.

Personally you are in favour of accepting the bid. You believe that the small size of your bank means that a takeover is inevitable. You want to recommend this offer to your shareholders. You believe that you and your colleagues have a much better chance of keeping your jobs after the takeover, or getting equivalent jobs in the new organization, if you consider it as a friendly bid.

Unit 18, Practice 1 Role A: The supplier

You want:

- to deliver 500 identical workstations
- to sell the workstations at $1,500 each
- payment within 30 days of delivery
- to deliver the equipment in 28 days
- to offer a six-month guarantee
- to have a long-term maintenance contract
- no guarantee concerning the price of further workstations ordered at a later date.

Unit 20 Role A: The bank

You want:

- to keep all branches open one hour longer on weekdays, until 5 pm
- to open 25 of your branches on Saturdays from 10 am to 2 pm
- to create 25 new jobs (or 50 part-time ones) as a result of this
- to reduce the working week from 39 to 37 hours for all staff who work on Saturdays
- to send all customer service staff on two training courses; each course will run for three days (Thursday–Saturday)
- to replace all existing employment contracts with new ones specifying a working week that can include Saturday
- to offer all staff an annual bonus if sales of banking products increase following the extension of opening hours.

As you prepare, think about what you will say in the meeting. What are your minimum requirements? What compromises would you be prepared to make? Which demands from the other side are unacceptable? Then negotiate – and see if you can come to an agreement.

Unit 18, Practice 2 Role A: The bank

You work for MGS Bank and you have called a meeting with the management team of Capper Trading.

The bank is considering granting the loan, depending on the conditions the company accepts. However, you think there is a considerable risk involved. If the toys stop selling, the company could have paid for 100,000 unwanted imported toys, on top of the 20,000 a week it is manufacturing itself. Under these conditions, you need to charge a high interest rate, and prefer an arrangement that gives you greater security.

You are prepared to offer EITHER a three-month loan at 3% (i.e. 12% per annum), which could be renewed or renegotiated if the product continues to sell, OR a one-year 9% loan that is secured by specified assets: if the company cannot repay the loan, you can oblige them to sell some of their assets, including their machinery and the factory they are in.

You would add a penalty clause: 1.2% per month for any loan not repaid on time.

You would charge your standard arrangement fee for loans over £50,000, which is 1.25%, plus a standard prepayment fee, which is 1% of the amount lent.

You would require the company to provide up-to-date sales figures to the bank every two weeks.

You want to know if the company has any plans to deal with negative changes in the exchange rate with the Chinese Yuan.

You also need some reassurance that the wholesalers Capper Trading are using to distribute the product are reliable and will pay their bills on time.

The bank must decide what it is prepared to offer, and under what conditions.

Unit 21 Role A: Investment advisor

You have a meeting with a very difficult client. He / She is a self-employed English language trainer who has written a Business English book, and who wrongly thinks he / she knows everything about finance. He / She does not have a huge amount of money – only £100,000. Being self-employed, your client will have no professional pension on retirement, and so cannot afford to take risks with his / her capital.

The client has sent you an email saying he / she wants you to sell all his / her bonds as the return isn't high enough, and to buy US stocks and / or call options, as the market is rising. At the same time he / she wants to speculate on the dollar continuing to fall in value, by buying put options. He / She also wants to buy commodity futures.

In the meeting you will have to explain to your client that:

- He / She should keep most of his / her capital in high quality bonds, because he / she will need this capital on retirement and so cannot take risks.
- You agree that the US stock market is rising, but think it is safer to diversify by investing a little in a tracker fund linked to the Dow-Jones Industrial Average (which consists of 30 of the largest companies in the US).
- You agree that it is a good time to buy US shares as the dollar has been falling and is currently low.
- Most analysts expect the dollar to start rising again, so this is not the time to speculate on it continuing to fall.
- If you <u>did</u> expect the dollar to continue to fall, it would not be a good idea to buy US stocks, as they would be worth less in your currency if you had to sell them.
- You do <u>not</u> think investing (or speculating) in commodities is a good idea as one can easily lose a lot of money this way.

You have a graph to show the client. It shows the volatility of stock markets, specifically how the major stock price index in your country has gone up and down over the past 25 years. This is to demonstrate that it is unsafe to invest only in stocks. You can explain the chart to your client, using some of the language for describing trends and graphs in **Unit 13**.

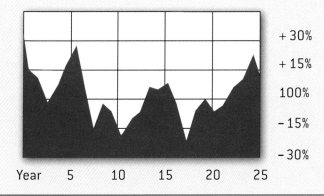

Unit 12, Practice 2 Role E: Finance Director

You are having a meeting with the Chief Executive (who is the Chair), the Human Resources Director, the Head of Customer Services and the Public Relations Director.

You would be totally in favour of the proposal if someone could provide you with a proposed budget with detailed costs that you could analyse.

If it could be demonstrated that outsourcing to India was profitable, and that Indian computer staff are more qualified and efficient, you would also recommend subcontracting your internet banking service and all your other computing jobs to India.

Unit 17, Practice 2 Role E: Risk Director

In this meeting you have to decide what to recommend to the shareholders: accept the bid, wait for a better one, or try to remain independent. At the end of the meeting, you will need to make a decision which will then be passed on to the Board.

You think the bank should accept the takeover on condition that it can continue to do business under its existing name (MGS Bank), as part of a larger financial group. Being part of a larger group would provide more capital and safety for your bank. As it is, the small size of your bank means that it is vulnerable to bad debts. The takeover might also allow you, the current managers, to get more interesting, higher-level jobs in the larger organization. You are opposed to any ideas involving issuing new shares to frighten off a takeover, as this could have unpredictable long-term consequences for the bank.

Unit 1 Role B

Call 1: The customer

You are interested in opening an 'e-saver' account and you want to know about the terms and conditions. Call the bank and ask questions to find out more information, and complete the table below.

	e-saver	Regular saver
Minimum deposit to open account		£1
Telephone / internet banking		✓
Overdraft facility		✓
Instant access to funds		✓
Higher interest rate for higher balances		✓
Minimum deposit each month		£500
Monthly statements		✓
Arrange transactions (e.g. bill payments) online		✗
ATM card		✓

Call 2: The bank

Now you work at the bank's call centre, answering customers' enquiries. A customer calls asking for more information about the 'regular saver' account. Use the information above to answer the customer's questions.

Unit 2, Practice 1 Role B: Robin Black in Retail Banking

You are taking part in a conference call with Kim Brown, the Assistant to Jean Chance, the Risk Manager. Kim wants you to attend a meeting with the Risk Manager. This is your schedule for tomorrow morning:

	HOLIDAY STARTS TODAY
08.30	Pick up plane tickets at travel agent as soon as they open
09.00	Call in at office for quick meeting with Chris in Mergers & Acquisitions
09.40	Leave for airport, taxi booked
10.00	
10.30	

Unit 2, Practice 2 Role B: Training manager

You work in the Training Department of an international company. You receive a call from a student about the company's International Graduate Training Programme. Give the following information in answer to the caller's questions:

- It's a two-year training programme for university graduates.
- It includes two foreign placements in countries where the company has offices; the main part of the programme is based in the head office in Cambridge.
- Candidates need a good university degree, a good level of English and two other languages.
- Trainees are paid £28,000, and are eligible for a performance-related bonus at the end of the first and second year of up to 25% of the base salary.
- The company covers the cost of trainees' accommodation during the programme up to the sum of £6,000 per annum.
- The company also offers private international healthcare and pension contributions.
- Interested graduates need to fill in the application form on the International Graduates page of the company's website at www.interprod.net, or write to The International Graduate Training Programme, International Products Limited, PO Box 4365, Cambridge CB31 2BU.

Unit 3 Role B: Head of Internet Banking

You have very different views to the Head of Retail Operations. You believe that within a few years online banking will inevitably lead to the closure of most branches. People will only use their internet connection and/or the telephone, and cash dispensers, and will hardly ever need to go into a branch. Even if some customers today prefer going to branches, you think this will not continue: these are mostly older people who have never used computers, and this will not be the case in the future. Consequently you think that any money spent on improving branch services will be wasted. The bank's IT staff do not need offices in expensive locations like high streets or shopping malls.

You can add any other examples and evidence that you can think of to support your argument.

Unit 4 Role B: Researcher 2

Your department is doing some internet research on mortgages. Your colleague calls to give you some useful web addresses. Write the addresses down.

Then suggest that your colleague looks at the following web pages. You will need to spell out the addresses.

http://ideas.repec.org/a/aea/jecper/v12y1998i2p41-62.html

http://www.businessweek.com/magazine/content/06_37/b4000001.htm

Give your colleague the following email address too:

resource_center@fanniemae.com

Unit 5, Practice 1 Role B: Bank team member

You are part of a team on the bank's training course. Look at the summaries of two loan applications below; summarize them to the other team members and listen to their summaries. Then discuss all the applications in your team, and make a preliminary recommendation in each case: do you think the bank should make the loan or not? Remember that riskier loans can be more profitable for the bank, but after a certain point, the risk of default or non-payment becomes too great.

Finally, put the loans you think the bank should grant in order of priority.

Case 4	Decision: Yes / No	Priority: ____
Your bank has been invited to join a syndicate lending $400 million dollars for the construction of a huge road bridge. A $10 toll for crossing the bridge, and the volume of traffic expected, would allow the promoter to repay the construction costs within 20 years. You are aware that the budgets for major civil engineering projects often seem to be wrong, and the final cost is often double the original estimation.		

Case 5	Decision: Yes / No	Priority: ____
Two hotel school graduates who have specialized in restaurant management want to borrow $20,000 to pay the franchise fee to open a new branch of a well-known, profitable and expanding international fast food chain. They expect to be able to repay the loan within two years.		

Unit 5, Practice 2 Role B: Customer
Meeting 1

You are one of the customers in Case 2 of **Practice 1** (see below) and you have been having a meeting with the bank advisor, who has just granted your loan. Before you end the meeting, the bank advisor wants to talk to you about other accounts and services the bank can offer. Listen and ask questions.

Case 2	Decision: Yes
Two garage mechanics want to set up their own small car repair business. They are confident that they will have enough customers. They both have 20 years' experience as car mechanics, working for somebody else, but no experience of running a business. But as they point out, nobody has this experience until they run their first business! They want to borrow $50,000, paying back $10,000 a year for five years.	

Unit 5, Practice 2 Role B: Bank customer advisor
Meeting 2

You have been having a meeting with one of the customers in Case 5 of **Practice 1** (see below) and you have just granted the loan. Before you end the meeting, you want to advise the customer to transfer all their accounts to your bank, and recommend that they use appropriate products and services from your bank. Use the information in the web page below.

Case 5	**Decision:** Yes

Two hotel school graduates who have specialized in restaurant management want to borrow $20,000 to pay the franchise fee to open a new branch of a well-known, profitable and expanding international fast food chain. They expect to be able to repay the loan within two years.

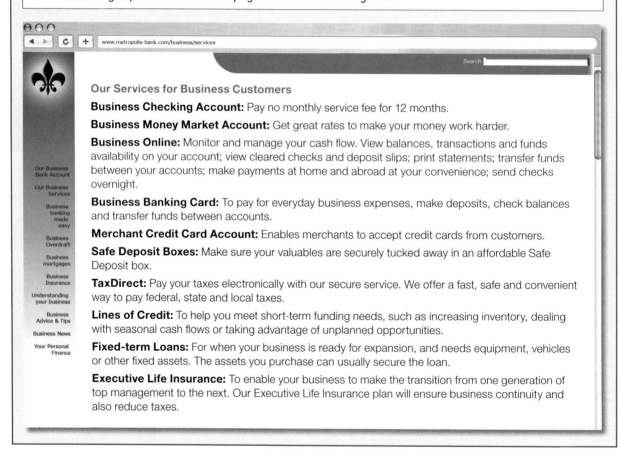

www.metropolis-bank.com/business/services

Search

Our Services for Business Customers

Business Checking Account: Pay no monthly service fee for 12 months.

Business Money Market Account: Get great rates to make your money work harder.

Business Online: Monitor and manage your cash flow. View balances, transactions and funds availability on your account; view cleared checks and deposit slips; print statements; transfer funds between your accounts; make payments at home and abroad at your convenience; send checks overnight.

Business Banking Card: To pay for everyday business expenses, make deposits, check balances and transfer funds between accounts.

Merchant Credit Card Account: Enables merchants to accept credit cards from customers.

Safe Deposit Boxes: Make sure your valuables are securely tucked away in an affordable Safe Deposit box.

TaxDirect: Pay your taxes electronically with our secure service. We offer a fast, safe and convenient way to pay federal, state and local taxes.

Lines of Credit: To help you meet short-term funding needs, such as increasing inventory, dealing with seasonal cash flows or taking advantage of unplanned opportunities.

Fixed-term Loans: For when your business is ready for expansion, and needs equipment, vehicles or other fixed assets. The assets you purchase can usually secure the loan.

Executive Life Insurance: To enable your business to make the transition from one generation of top management to the next. Our Executive Life Insurance plan will ensure business continuity and also reduce taxes.

Sidebar navigation:
Our Business Bank Account
Our Business Services
Business banking made easy
Business Overdraft
Business mortgages
Business Insurance
Understanding your business
Business Advice & Tips
Business News
Your Personal Finance

Unit 8, Practice 1 Role B
Meeting 1: Visitor

You are Pat Brown. Someone you have not met before comes to meet you at the reception desk of a company you are visiting. Greet your host, introduce yourself, and answer the questions you are asked. Then ask a couple of questions to keep the conversation going.

Meeting 2: Host

You are Kim Green. A business partner, Robin White, is visiting your offices and you have just finished your first meeting. While you are having a coffee, ask your visitor where they live, where they come from originally, their family, their hobbies, etc.

Ask if they are doing anything this evening, and whether they would like to join you for dinner.

Unit 8, Practice 3 Role B: Host

You have been having lunch with people from another company after a meeting, but now they have to leave. You have arranged a taxi to the airport for them, which will pick them up outside the hotel. You will be seeing them next month when you go to Paris.

Unit 10 Student B

You can arrange a special tour of the stock exchange and the central bank in the capital city. The tour would cost £150, and transport to the capital would be £40 per person by train, or £260 to hire a minibus and driver for the day. If the second option was chosen, you would like to add an evening's entertainment as well. You will ask the meeting for suggestions.

Unit 11 Role B: Advisor

You work in a bank's call centre, answering customer enquiries. An inexperienced exporter calls you wanting to know more about Incoterms. Use the bank's web page and the information below to answer the customer's questions.

FAS (Free Alongside Ship) means that the seller's bill only includes delivering the goods to the port. The buyer pays for loading the goods onto the ship (as well as for the transportation by ship). With FOB (Free On Board), the seller pays for loading the goods onto the ship, and includes this in the price.

DEQ (Delivered Ex Quay) means that the seller's price includes the cost of unloading the goods from the ship at the port of arrival. DES (Delivered Ex Ship) means that the buyer pays for this on top of the amount paid to the seller. This is a similar distinction to the one between FAS and FOB.

The exporter can choose which Incoterm to use; these specify who pays for the insurance. With the E and F terms, the buyer is responsible for insurance. With the D terms, the seller arranges and pays for insurance. With the C terms there is a choice: in CIF and CIP the seller is responsible for insurance, with CFR and CPT insurance is the buyer's responsibility.

DDU and DDP no not apply to goods exported from one European Union country to another, because there are no import duties among member countries. If the seller chooses to use one of the D terms, it would be DAF, DES or DEQ.

Unit 12, Practice 1 Student B

You have the following opinions. Take turns – express one of the opinions to your partner, ask what his / her opinions are on the topic, and agree or disagree. Then listen to one of your partner's opinions, and agree or disagree.

- Company directors shouldn't earn more than $1m a year.
- Free markets work and governments should never intervene.
- Mothers shouldn't work but should stay at home with their children.
- People should be allowed to live in any country they like.
- There should be a 40% tax on capital gains.
- There's no proof that global warming is happening.
- There's no future for manufacturing industry in Western countries.
- Most people like to have responsibility at work.

Unit 12, Practice 2 Role B: Human Resources Director

You are having a meeting with the Chief Executive (who is the Chair), the Head of Customer Services, the Public Relations Director and the Finance Director.

You are against this proposal, for the following reasons:

Following UK branch closures due to the growth of internet and telephone banking, there have already been heavy job losses. Staff morale is very low and you are concerned that further cuts could affect productivity.

Your British staff are directly employed by the bank, unlike the proposed new employees, who will be working for a subcontractor.

A recent national consumer survey gave the bank a high score for customer service, and you are reluctant to do anything to damage this good record.

You are also worried about the security aspects of giving an outside company online access to your customers' data.

Unit 15, Practice 1 Student B

Describe the changes in the share prices of the Sumitomo Mitsui Banking Corporation to your partner using the graph below. Do not let your partner see your graph.

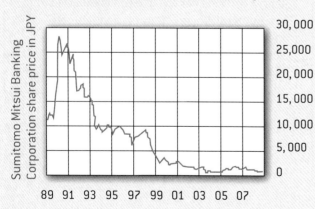

Now draw the graph that your partner describes to you.

Unit 17, Practice 2 Role B: Head of Corporate Banking

In this meeting you have to decide what to recommend to the shareholders: accept the bid, wait for a better one, or try to remain independent. At the end of the meeting, you will need to make a decision which will then be passed on to the Board.

You think that the small size of your bank makes a takeover almost inevitable sooner or later. But since nearly all large commercial banks are trying to get bigger by acquiring smaller banks, you have no reason to recommend accepting this particular offer. You can wait for a better one. You think you should refuse and look for a 'white knight' – another bidder who you prefer. You suggest contacting other large banks and offering to merge with them on condition that they allow you to keep the bank's name – and your jobs.

Unit 18, Practice 1 Role B: The bank

You want:

- to have three slightly different models of workstation
- to pay between $1,300 and $1,450 for each workstation
- delivery of the equipment within two weeks of your order
- to pay 90 days after delivery
- a one-year guarantee
- to use another company for maintenance
- an option to buy 200 more workstations at the same price next year.

Unit 20 Role B: The staff association

You want:

- only voluntary agreements to work on Saturdays
- no changed contracts; employees who agree to Saturday working will give their written consent
- a full weekday off to compensate for Saturday working
- the possibility for all staff to work a four-day week (even those not working on Saturday)
- a reduction in the working week from 39 to 35 hours, to compensate for the extra hour a day (4–5 pm) spent with customers
- a rise of one grade in the pay scale for all staff who complete the customer service training courses, or a monthly payment of £150
- two weekdays off for each Saturday spent on a training course
- to retrain four members of staff from the Trade Finance department (made redundant by internet banking) for four of the new jobs, if the plan goes ahead.

As you prepare, think about what you will say in the meeting. What are your minimum requirements? What compromises would you be prepared to make? Which demands from the other side are unacceptable? Then negotiate – and see if you can come to an agreement.

Unit 18, Practice 2 Role B: The customer

You are one of the management team at Capper Trading and you have been called to a meeting at MGS Bank.

You are convinced that you have a wonderful commercial opportunity. You are a small manufacturing and trading company that has obtained merchandising rights for toys linked to a children's cartoon series. You have this contract because of family connections with the producers of the series, but this is not information you need to share with the bank.

You have no idea how many toys you are going to be able to sell, but it is potentially *millions*, because the cartoon series is going to be sold to television companies all round the world, and you have exclusive rights.

As long as sales are increasing, you will need credit to pay the Chinese sub-contracted manufacturers for their products, while you wait for payment from your wholesalers. This should only be a short-term credit (30–60 days) for each order, as you expect payment within this period.

When the number of sales (and the number of products made) stops growing, but stays at the same level, you will soon become self-financing, but you do not know when this will happen.

You have come to MGS Bank because they have several branches in your city, and their advertising states that they want to help local businesses. If your new product is as successful as you think it is going to be, it will be good for the bank's reputation if they work with you.

You are ordering 100,000 units at a time from China. You need an initial loan of £400,000 for three months, and probably more after that. Ideally, you need an unlimited credit line for about a year.

You do not think there is any risk attached to this loan, and do not see why you should pay a high interest rate. You know that MGS Bank's base rate (for their biggest and safest business customers) is 6%. You are prepared to pay 7.5% fixed interest, and a 1% arrangement fee for the loan, but will ask for a loan at 6%.

First prepare your role in a small group: what will your team say in the meeting? The company must decide what it wants, and what it is prepared to accept.

Unit 21 Role B: Client

You are going to a meeting with your investment advisor to discuss what you want him / her to do with your money. You have £100,000, most of it from a best-selling Business English book. As well as writing the book, you have been training business people for many years, and so know quite a lot about business and finance – you think you probably know more than the rather inexperienced advisor responsible for your account. You are annoyed that the bank does not seem to consider you as an important investor, and want to tell them that you will take your money somewhere else. You could join a hedge fund for example, or trade stocks or currency online without using a bank.

But for the moment, you want to give the bank a chance to get you a return of 15–20% on your money. You want:

- to sell all your bonds, as the interest rate is very low
- to put most of your money in two or three US stocks, and / or call options, because US stocks seem to be rising; you expect your advisor to recommend which ones
- to buy some put options to sell US dollars in three months' time, as this currency is falling
- to buy some commodity futures; you expect your advisor to recommend which ones.

You have two graphs which you have cut out of newspapers, and you want to show these to your advisor. You can explain what has happened to these possible assets using some of the language for describing trends and graphs in **Unit 13**. You feel that your advisor doesn't listen to you, so you will have to explain what you want quite firmly.

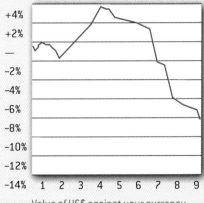

Value of US$ against your currency for the last 9 months

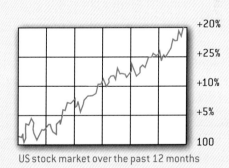

US stock market over the past 12 months

Unit 2, Practice 1 Role D: Chris White in Mergers & Acquisitions

You are taking part in a conference call with Kim Brown, the Assistant to Jean Chance, the Risk Manager. Kim wants you to attend a meeting with the Risk Manager. This is your schedule for tomorrow morning:

09.00	Meeting with Robin Black, Retail Banking
09.30	Interviewing candidate for financial accounting job
10.00	
10.30–11.00	Meeting with Jean Chance, Risk Manager, and Lee Rock, the Chief Executive

Unit 5, Practice 1 Role D: Bank team member

You are part of a team on the bank's training exercise. Look at the summaries of two loan applications below; summarize them to the other team members and listen to their summaries. Then discuss all the applications in your team, and make a preliminary recommendation in each case: do you think the bank should make the loan or not? Remember that riskier loans can be more profitable for the bank, but after a certain point, the risk of default or non-payment becomes too great.

Finally, put the loans you think the bank should grant in order of priority.

Case 3	Decision: Yes / No	Priority: ___
A 50-year-old national airline, currently losing millions of dollars a year, is undergoing a major restructuring, but needs to borrow $50 million dollars. Your bank has been invited to join a syndicate and lend $5 million for an indefinite period. The airline's credit rating has just been downgraded from BB to B.		

Case 8	Decision: Yes / No	Priority: ___
A local manufacturing company employing 30 people has not been paid for a large export order. The order was insured by a government export credit guarantee, but this will not be paid for six to nine months. The company needs to borrow $500,000 for this period.		

Unit 10 Student D

You want to continue doing what the bank has done for several years, and hire an expert to give a series of seven 90-minute seminars on finance and banking. These are usually on Friday afternoons, when the trainees find it hard to concentrate, so this year you want to schedule them at 8.00 or 8.30 on Monday mornings. You pay the lecturer £80 per session. Before the meeting you heard colleagues suggesting other non-serious forms of 'training', such as watching films, and you are totally against such proposals. You intend to make your views extremely clear.

Unit 12, Practice 2 Role D: Public Relations Director

You are having a meeting with the Chief Executive (who is the Chair), the Human Resources Director, the Head of Customer Services and the Finance Director.

You are against this proposal, for the following reasons:

It will mean dismissing 50 British workers in a small town in which you are one of the larger employers. Your organization has recently had a great deal of press coverage about closures to local branches and job losses. You are concerned that an announcement of further job cuts could have a damaging effect on the image of your company.

After some of your biggest competitors were taken over by foreign banks, your advertising used slogans about your bank being British. Moving your telephone banking service to India would make your advertising seem dishonest.

You are also concerned that customers may find speaking to call centre staff in another country too impersonal, and feel that they prefer discussing their accounts with UK-based staff who have local knowledge.

Unit 17, Practice 2 Role D: Human Resources Director

In this meeting you have to decide what to recommend to the shareholders: accept the bid, wait for a better one, or try to remain independent. At the end of the meeting, you will need to make a decision which will then be passed on to the Board.

You believe that your bank's success is due to its regional character. Customers open savings accounts with you because they know that the money is being lent to local businesses. If the bank is taken over and becomes part of another bank, your customers will have no reason to stay with you. Furthermore, the new owners could choose to close many of your branches – many of which are currently being modernized – and ask your customers to transfer to their existing branches. This could lead to many jobs being lost. You recommend refusing the takeover offer. You also believe that the bank should frighten off the 'predator' with a 'poison pill' defence: you should let all your existing shareholders (except the bank trying to acquire you) buy an enormous number of newly issued shares at a large discount. This would make the cost of buying the company much higher and reduce or dilute the value of the shares the predator already holds.

Unit 2, Practice 1 Role C: Pat Green in Corporate Banking

You are taking part in a conference call with Kim Brown, the Assistant to Jean Chance, the Risk Manager. Kim wants you to attend a meeting with the Risk Manager. This is your schedule for tomorrow morning:

08.45	Giving introductory talk to 10 new trainees
09.15	Meeting with Lee Rock, the bank's Chief Executive; probably 90 minutes
11.00	
11.30	
12.00	

Unit 3 Role C: Head of Retail Operations

You have very different views to the Head of Internet Banking. You believe that recent research shows that attractive branches bring in customers who will buy more banking products. You expect that a majority of customers will always prefer to go to a bank branch. You want to invest substantially in relocating branches in shopping centres, and redesigning them – making them friendlier, selling refreshments, opening longer hours, and so on. You would like larger counselling areas, where financial advisors could recommend banking products and services to customers, and deal with their problems.

You can also mention any negative aspects of internet banking that you can think of.

Unit 5, Practice 1 Role C: Bank team member

You are part of a team on the bank's training exercise. Look at the summaries of two loan applications below; summarize them to the other team members and listen to their summaries. Then discuss all the applications in your team, and make a preliminary recommendation in each case: do you think the bank should make the loan or not? Remember that riskier loans can be more profitable for the bank, but after a certain point, the risk of default or non-payment becomes too great.

Finally, put the loans you think the bank should grant in order of priority.

Case 2	Decision: Yes / No	Priority: ____

Two garage mechanics want to set up their own small car repair business. They are confident that they will have enough customers. They both have 20 years' experience as car mechanics, working for somebody else, but no experience of running a business. But as they point out, nobody has this experience until they run their first business! They want to borrow $50,000, paying back $10,000 a year for five years.

Case 7	Decision: Yes / No	Priority: ____

A football club in a medium-sized town needs €300,000 instantly, to pay the staff and players' salaries. The club, which has previously been successful, is looking for new investors and sponsors and expects to find them soon. In case of bankruptcy, the land on which the stadium is built would be worth more than the club's debts.

Unit 10 Student C

You think the trainees would appreciate something relaxing after a hard day's work. You would like to hire or buy DVDs of films about finance, show them to the trainees, and discuss the issues involved. You suggest *Wall Street*, a well-known movie about financial crime, and *Rogue Trader*, about the collapse of Barings Bank in 1995. You will ask your colleagues to suggest other films. This option would be very cheap, and enjoyable.

Unit 12, Practice 2
Role C: Head of Customer Services

You are having a meeting with the Chief Executive (who is the Chair), the Human Resources Director, the Public Relations Director and the Finance Director.

You are in favour of this proposal, for the following reasons:

You have done market research which shows that your customers are quite happy to do their telephone banking with staff based in other regions of the UK.

You expect that the staff in the Indian companies are far more educated and competent than many of the telephone staff you currently employ in Britain.

You think that everybody will gain from this deal: the bank, its customers, and the employees of the Indian company you will be working with.

You are tired of listening to some of your colleagues' weak arguments against this proposal, and so you tend to interrupt them.

Unit 17, Practice 2
Role C: Head of Retail Operations

In this meeting you have to decide what to recommend to the shareholders: accept the bid, wait for a better one, or try to remain independent. At the end of the meeting, you will need to make a decision which will then be passed on to the Board.

You are strongly opposed to recommending the takeover. You believe that your personal customers have chosen your bank because of its local reputation. They like the bank because they feel it belongs to their region, even though most of the shares are owned by institutional investors in the capital city. You do not see any advantages in becoming part of a larger financial services group, whose shareholders have no connection to your region. You do not think that you should be discussing how best to save your particular jobs – the issue is much more important than that.

Unit 22 Presentation A

You are describing your organization, or another company that you know well, to potential job applicants at a university job fair.

The presentation should include:

- a brief history of the company
- its current operations
- its prospects for the future.

Unit 22 Presentation B

You are an executive director of a financial organization reporting to the non-executive directors on the Board on how you see the future of your sector of the financial industry.

The presentation should outline:

- how the sector operates now
- what changes you foresee in the future
- how you think the organization should start preparing for them now.

Unit 22 Presentation C

You are reporting on your company's recent performance to shareholders, stock analysts or the media.

You could talk about:

- sales revenue
- pre-tax and net profit
- the evolution of the share price
- dividends paid
- shareholders' equity
- available cash.

Tapescripts

1.1 Types of banks

Peter Sinclair: Well, twenty-five years ago the financial industry in most countries had two key characteristics. One was that pretty well all the banks and financial institutions in that country were owned in that country, and there were few international links – in many cases none. So they were national banks belonging to that country. The other key feature was that financial institutions were specialized, so in Britain we had institutions that lent to people who wanted to borrow to buy houses – that means arranging mortgages – so we had specialized things called building societies doing that. We had retail banks where individuals and companies kept bank deposits and which made loans to cover short-term outlays and in some cases longer-term investment. Then we had another range of institutions like insurance companies to provide life insurance or pensions, and we had investment banks – sometimes called merchant banks. These weren't retail banks; they didn't deal with individuals, they dealt with big companies. They gave the companies financial advice, maybe arranging mergers, or fighting off a takeover bid, and helped to raise capital, for example by issuing shares or bonds.

1.2 Going international

Peter Sinclair: In the old days in Britain, the merchant or investment banks were pretty well all British and there were big boundaries between building societies and insurance companies and all these other types of companies. Well, now if you look at the picture, many banks have become universal banks; perhaps 'banks' is the wrong word. Lots of institutions do all the things that I have just described – insurance, mortgages, advice, raising capital for companies, and retail banking besides, and the other great change is that so many of the financial institutions – and it is not just true of Britain, true of pretty much everywhere else – are now international. So, for example in Britain, two of the big four retail banks have changed ownership: one was taken over by Hong Kong and Shanghai Bank, that was the Midland Bank previously, and it's now changed its name to Hong Kong and Shanghai Bank and it really isn't a British bank any more; and another, National Westminster, was taken over by the Royal Bank of Scotland. But if you look at, say, countries like the Czech Republic or Hungary or Poland or New Zealand too, and plenty of other small countries around the world, all their financial institutions pretty well are now owned by foreigners, by German companies, or French companies or Austrian companies – whatever it might be – and the huge international financial institutions are typically, though not all of them, American; and you can now think of the City of London, the world's leading centre for foreign exchange dealings and a great deal of finance, as rather like Wimbledon. In other words it's a great big international stage, happens to be in London, but most of the players are foreign; they are nearly all foreign companies that do, for example, the investment banking and so many other things.

So internationalization and, if you like, homogenization of these hitherto specialized financial institutions. Those are the two big recent trends.

2.1 Arranging meetings

Call 1

Pat:	... I'm not sure that's possible. You know, Kim, I think we should have a meeting about this.
Kim:	Sure. Are you free on Thursday?
Pat:	Let me just check my diary. Sorry, I'm busy on Thursday. Is Friday OK?
Kim:	Yes. How about nine o'clock?
Pat:	Yes, nine o'clock is fine. Your office or mine?
Kim:	Oh, I'll come to your office if you like.
Pat:	OK, see you on Friday at nine in my office.
Kim:	OK. See you then.

Call 2

Pat:	Hello, Pat again. Something's come up. I have to go to Head Office on Friday. Can we make it next Monday instead?
Kim:	No, sorry, I can't manage Monday, clients all day. Can you do Tuesday?
Pat:	Sorry, Tuesday's not convenient. I'm busy non-stop. How about Wednesday?
Kim:	OK, let's say eleven o'clock. Would that suit you?
Pat:	Yes, that's fine, Wednesday at eleven. I'll come over to you. Sorry to mess you around like this.
Kim:	No problem. I'll confirm that by email.
Pat:	It's OK, I don't need an email – I'll be there. Bye.

2.2 Handling information

Customer:	Hello, this is Mr Kolodziejczyk. I have a current account and a mortgage with you, and I'm calling for some information about loans.
Bank:	Yes Mr Kolo ..., yes sir, what would you like to know?
Customer:	I'd like to borrow £25,000 to buy a boat, and I'd like to know what interest rate you'd charge.
Bank:	Well, our personal loans currently have a typical annual rate of six point four percent.
Customer:	Six point four, yes. But could you tell me about secured loans? I read something somewhere about them being cheaper.
Bank:	Yes, of course. That's right. If the loan is secured against a home, a life assurance policy or another suitable asset, the typical annual rate is only five percent. What type of security do you have in mind? Your home?
Customer:	Yes, I've nearly paid off my mortgage.
Bank:	That would probably be acceptable. And the loan can be for any term up to twenty years. When and how are you thinking of paying back?
Customer:	Well, I'm not sure. I would probably want to repay capital and interest together each month. But it depends. Maybe I'd prefer to pay the interest only, and to repay the capital after five or six years.
Bank:	OK. Perhaps it would be better if I sent you an application form for a secured loan. Could you give me your name again?
Customer:	Kolodziejczyk. That's K-O-L-O-D-Z-I-E-J-C-Z-Y-K. It's Polish.
Bank:	Yes, thank you. And your first name?
Customer:	Stephen. Well actually it's Szczepan – S-Z-C-Z-E-P-A-N – but these days I spell it S-T-E-P-H-E-N. You have my address. I'm sure I'm the only Stephen Kolodziejczyk at your branch. But can I leave you a new mobile number? It's zero seven eight, nine one nine, double three seven two.

3   Retail banking

Peter Sinclair: Well, I'm not sure that retail banking is declining. I think in many countries the size of bank deposits, that's the liabilities that the retail banks have, has been growing faster than national income – it's been rising. People are increasingly moving away from currency towards things like bank deposits, that's a slow gradual trend and it's a trend evident in most places, especially the more developing poorer countries, emerging economies and so on.

So I think retail banking has always been regarded as important, but perhaps a little boring for some people. So the real action seems to be more in the big-scale operations with large companies, in huge deals and other kinds of activity which are thought to be more sophisticated and perhaps more rewarding than retail banking. More sophisticated yes, more specialized yes, but not more lucrative, and often more dangerous. Retail banking I think is not in decline; although people have been predicting that it might be at some point, there's no evidence that it is.

5.1   Lending decisions

Interviewer: How do banks decide who to lend to?

Gerlinde Igler: Normally we analyse the customers. That means that we analyse the annual reports, the figures during the year. We have to analyse how the company will develop in the future. So we evaluate the current situation of the customer and the future situation of the customer.

We also discuss the loan with the customers – what kind of loan is it? Is it a short-term loan or is it a long-term loan? It's very important to know the maturity of this loan. If we lend money for a long time we have to be sure that the customer can repay this loan. Normally the company must be able to repay the loan from the operating cash flow, the EBIT of the company.

Our decision also depends on the bank's portfolio. We finance different sectors in industry, and we've got different limits for the sectors. And if we overstep this limit with the new customer, we need a new approval for the higher limit for the sector, and we have to decide if it's OK to increase the credit limit for the sector.

We also have a rating for each sector, and we have to decide if it is a sector with a good rating or a sector with a bad rating. If you have a sector with a bad rating we normally only finance the best companies in this sector.

Sometimes the customer would like to finance some different transactions in foreign countries. If we finance transactions in Eastern Europe or in Asia we have to look at the country rating and we have to look at the limit for this country. For these countries we have limits or we have no limits. If we don't have a limit for this country we can't finance it – it's too dangerous.

5.2   Margins

Gerlinde Igler: The last important point is that we would like to earn money with the customer [laughs]; we need an agreement about the margin. We have a special system, a special calculation system, in which we calculate the margin, and the margin is added to the cost of funds, and the cost of funds plus the margin is then the interest rate of the customers. We need an acceptable margin.

The cost of funds will depend on the market situation and the bank's rating. If you have a good rating you can get money on the capital markets more cheaply than a bank with a bad rating. Every bank is rated by the international agencies, Standard & Poor's and Moody's. It's a big disadvantage if you don't have a Triple A rating. You have to pay higher interest for the money you borrow.

We calculate a margin and the margin includes the product costs. The product costs depend on the product the customer will use. Then we have the overhead costs. Overhead costs depend on the situation of the bank. A smaller bank has a lot of overhead costs and a big bank normally has lower overhead costs.

The most important point is the risk costs, because the risk costs depend on the customer's rating. If I have a bad customer and the customer has a bad rating, in this case the customer has to pay a higher margin. If we can get securities or collateral we can reduce our risks, because we can use this collateral if the company goes bust.

But there is a lot of competition between the banks and it's very hard for small banks to get good customers or to get acceptable margins.

6.1   A letter of complaint

John:	Hello?
Charlotte:	Hi John, Charlotte here. I've got a very aggressive letter here I've got to answer, and I'd like a second opinion.
John:	OK ...
Charlotte:	We have a customer whose card was being used fraudulently, until it reached the credit limit. And she was on holiday on a small Hawaiian island and suddenly found her card didn't work, and didn't have any other way of getting cash.
John:	And we didn't notice anything until too late?
Charlotte:	Well, we did. It's someone ordering things from the internet, to be sent to an address in the States. We've now notified the authorities there and blocked the account. But this happened last year, and the transactions weren't fraudulent. At the time, we contacted the customer and she wrote an angry letter saying, 'Can't I buy presents for friends in America without getting stupid letters from my credit card company?' or something like that. This time, we noticed the transactions but didn't immediately do anything. So suddenly she was on the other side of the world with no money, and she couldn't pay the hotel, and she couldn't get to the airport, and she missed her flight, and so on, and she says it's all our fault.
John:	And she didn't have any other cards?
Charlotte:	Apparently not, and it took two days for her bank to transfer money to her. It was the weekend, there's a ten-hour time difference, she couldn't call her bank at night, and so on.
John:	Well, that's unfortunate. But we explain the situation, and tell her that we would have taken action sooner over suspected fraudulent transactions if she hadn't replied to us like that last year. Besides, if a card is being used fraudulently we have to block it, so she'd have been in the same situation anyway.
Charlotte:	True, but the thing is the customer in question is the daughter of the Chairman of MGS Bank. She makes quite sure she tells us that in her letter.
John:	[laughs] And he couldn't get money to her for two days?
Charlotte:	Apparently not to Hawaii.
John:	What about her MGS Bank debit card?
Charlotte:	I think she'd reached her limit on that.

John:	Well, that's not our fault, is it? Adapt the standard letter, you know, regretting the inconvenience, say we're doing everything we can to prevent fraud, etc., but absolutely not admitting liability. Show it to me before you send it, if you like.
Charlotte:	OK, thanks.

6.2   An angry phone call

Customer:	Is that MGS Bank? My name's Hewson and I work at Green's, the garden centre. The police just came round to my house, on my day off, and I was nearly arrested! And it's all your fault, because you haven't got a night safe. I want to speak to the branch manager. Now!
Bank employee:	I'm sorry, Mr Hewson, I can't put you through to the manager at the moment. You'll have to explain the situation to me.
Customer:	I just did! There were two policemen at my house! Accusing me!
Bank employee:	Mr Hewson, if you could just try to calm down a little and explain the situation to me. I'm not quite sure I follow you.
Customer:	I told you, it's your night safe. You can't use it. It's boarded over, because they're renovating the building. So I couldn't put the money in it yesterday afternoon.
Bank employee:	Yes, Mr Hewson, we are renovating the building, and work has been going on for three weeks now. And we notified all our customers about this a long time ago. Now perhaps you could explain exactly what the problem is? Did you take some money home instead of depositing it?
Customer:	Yes, I already told you I couldn't deposit it.
Bank employee:	And this morning your manager checked the account, and the money wasn't there?
Customer:	Yes.
Bank employee:	And he notified the police?
Customer:	Yes.
Bank employee:	He didn't call you first?
Customer:	I don't know, my phone wasn't turned on. I told you, it's my day off.
Bank employee:	But you have the money?
Customer:	Yes.
Bank employee:	And you've explained this to the police? And your manager?
Customer:	Yes, but I don't like being woken up by the police accusing me of stealing fifteen hundred pounds because you don't have a night safe.
Bank employee:	Well, it's true that we don't have a night safe at present, but we do have an automated deposit machine in the self-service area of all our branches, next to the cash dispensers, where you can deposit both notes and coins, 24 hours a day. Are you sure your manager told you to use the night safe?
Customer:	Er, I don't know. But I still want to speak to the manager! Immediately!

7.1   Types of accounting

Eric Sharp:	In general, most of the boring work is done by purchase ledger clerks and sales ledger clerks. These are usually bookkeepers who are not qualified to a high level. The information they produce – which is basically a summary of transactions – can then be interpreted by management accountants. It can then be used by senior accountants at financial controller and director level, both for making decisions on the future of the business, and for advising other parts of the business on how to proceed.

The company's accountants also do an internal audit. The aim of this tends to be to ensure that management have sufficient internal control over what is going on. The aim of the external audit is to ensure that published financial statements give a true and fair view of the company's profit, and of its assets and liabilities.

7.2   Financial statements

Eric Sharp: There are three or four different statements that companies include in their Annual Reports, which shareholders can legally expect to see. The key documents are the profit and loss account, the balance sheet, and a funds flow statement of some kind. In the USA, and under International Financial Reporting Standards, the profit and loss account is called an income statement. This document is fairly self-explanatory: it's income less expenditure. The balance sheet is a statement showing what the company has, and what it owes at the end of the year, while the funds flow statement attempts to show whether the company is generating or consuming cash. The tax authorities require more detail than is given in these documents; taxable profit is not the same as accounting profit, so they will expect to see reconciliations between the two.

7.3   Barclays' balance sheet

Journalist: Large banks these days really do possess and manage vast sums of money. For example, Barclays' tangible assets – the buildings the banks are in, and so on, recorded in the accounts as property, plant and equipment – are only worth two point seven five four billion, but the group's total worth, or their shareholders' equity, is twenty-four point four three billion. Their total assets are nine hundred and twenty-four billion, three hundred and fifty-seven million pounds. Barclays' customers have deposited two hundred and thirty-eight billion, six hundred and eighty-four million pounds in their accounts, and the bank has advanced or lent its customers two hundred and sixty-eight billion, eight hundred and ninety-six million pounds. These really are huge figures.

8.1   Greeting people and making introductions

Michael: Excuse me, are you Mrs Steiner?

Monica: Yes. Hello.

Michael: Hi. I'm Michael. Welcome to New York.

Monica: How do you do? But please call me Monica.

Michael: Sure. Monica, do you know Siobhan?

Monica: Hello, nice to meet you.

Siobhan: Hi. How are you?

Monica: Fine, thanks. I'm sorry, I didn't catch your name.

Siobhan: Siobhan. It's Irish.

Michael: We have a car outside. Can I take your bag?

Monica: Thank you.

Siobhan: How was your flight? You must be tired.

Monica: No, I slept a little on the plane. I'm fine.

Siobhan: OK. Well, we'll take you to your hotel. Is this your first time in New York?

Monica: Oh no, I've been here a couple of times. But on vacation, not on business.

Michael: Not in November, I guess. I hope it's not too cold for you.

Monica: No, it's fine. It was almost the same in Zurich, actually.

8.2   Talking about your career

Michael: How long have you worked in the finance department at Head Office?

Monica: Two years. I applied for a job there in my last year at university, when I was studying finance and economics, but I didn't even get an interview. So I went to London and worked as a trainee in a British bank for six months. After that I joined a Swiss bank where I worked in the corporate department. Then I was transferred to their trade finance department. But I didn't get promoted so after three years I applied to this company again, and they offered me my present job. I really like what I'm doing now. I find financial planning really interesting. I'm responsible for some very big projects. What about you?

Michael: Well, I studied accounting at university and then worked for an auditing firm for two years, but I didn't like it. So I did an MBA, and then got a job here. Now, as you know, I'm in production and operations. I'm in charge of setting up new production facilities here, which is why I'm working on this project with you, and I'm also involved in two projects in Canada. Which means I'm always dealing with lots of problems at the same time. But I enjoy the challenge!

8.3   Saying goodbye

Monica: I'm afraid I have to go now, but it's been a very useful meeting.

Michael: Of course. Yes, it's been very interesting working with you.

Monica: And I look forward to seeing you in Zurich next month. You've got my card, but let me give you my mobile number. Have you got a pen? It's 074 433 ...

Michael: 074 433 ...

Monica: ... 1991. Got that?

Michael: 1991. Thanks. If you'd like to wait in reception, the taxi will pick you up from just outside.

Monica: Ah, good. Thanks for organizing that.

Michael: No problem. See you in Zurich. Goodbye, and have a good flight!

Monica: Thanks. Bye.

9.1   Monetary policy

Kate Barker: At the Bank of England, in common with most central banks round the world now, when we look at monetary policy, it involves changing interest rates.

The aim of monetary policy is to keep inflation low and stable. When you're setting interest rates, what you're trying to do is to keep demand in the economy, what people consume, how much they invest, in line with the long-term ability of an economy to supply goods and services through labour, through people employed, and through the capital employed, machinery, plant and equipment in the economy.

When interest rates rise, this will mean that individuals will tend to save more and consume less. Also for companies, investment decisions are more expensive and that means that demand will tend to be reduced. When interest rates are cut, the opposite happens – people will spend rather than save and companies have more of an incentive to invest, and that means that the level of demand rises. And it's by trying to set demand, to keep demand in line with supply in future, so that the central bank is always looking ahead.

When the central bank sets the base rate for lending to commercial banks, it affects the whole structure of interest rates in a country. For example, in the United Kingdom one of the things it affects very quickly is the rate at which the banks and other organizations lend to households for their mortgages, but of course it will also affect the rates at which companies borrow. Of course that just means that the central bank controls the short-term interest rate. What happens to other interest rates, one-year, five-year, ten-year interest rates, can be quite different.

9.2   Saying figures

1   They're buying euros at one point four four three five, and selling them at one point four nine three five.
2   So the spread is zero point oh five, or about three point four per cent.
3   The three-month dollar rate is two point seven five per cent.
4   Did you say eight hundred and eighteen point eight one eight?
5   No, you're not listening. I said eight hundred eighty point eight zero eight.
6   I can't read this – is it two hundred and four thousand, six hundred and eighty-three, or two hundred and four point six eight three?
7   He's very tall – two metres twelve – and most doors are only about two metres two centimetres high.
8   Our CEO earns about thirty-three cents a second. And there are thirty-one million, five hundred thirty-six thousand seconds in a year.
9   Really? Let me see. That's ten million, four hundred and six thousand, eight hundred and eighty dollars.
10   That's right. And that's two hundred forty-six point zero two five five three one nine times more than I earn!

10.1   Chairing a meeting

Chair: Hello, everybody. Thank you all for coming. It's nine o'clock so let's get started. This morning we're meeting to discuss all the financial aspects of moving our call centres to India. As you'll have seen, this is the main item on today's agenda.

Unfortunately, we've received apologies from Fernando Montero, our Computing Systems Director. He's stranded at an airport somewhere because of fog, so I'm afraid we'll have to continue without him.

You've all received the minutes of our last meeting. Are there any matters arising? ... OK, if no one has any comments, I'll move on to the next item and ask Alice Hewlett, Head of Customer Services, to report on her trip to India.

Alice Hewlett: Thank you. As you know, I went to Hyderabad and Bangalore last week to talk to two companies ...

10.2   Interruptions and digressions

Alice Hewlett: So, as I was saying, because the staff of both companies already speak excellent English, and have already had intensive courses about British culture, they only need to learn about our bank, and our products and services. Consequently, training costs would be very low ...

Susan: Yeah, but you're forgetting the cost of laying off all our call centre staff in Britain.

Chair: Susan, you didn't let Alice finish.

Alice Hewlett: Thank you. I'd like to add that I was easily able to find out that the starting salary for call centre staff in both cities is about 8,000 rupees a month, although the average salary is about 10,000 rupees, which is about $220. So I think that both quotes we've had are rather high, and we can easily negotiate with the companies concerned ...

Susan: Well, I'm not at all convinced it's a good thing to have our customers' phone calls answered by people who work for a subcontractor, rather than by bank staff. I think a lot of people feel this way, and this could give us a lot of bad publicity. I also think ...

Chair:	I'm sorry, Susan, but that's not the question we're considering today. We're talking about the financial implications of contracting out our telephone operations. Does anyone have anything else to add on this topic? No? Well, Alice, can I just summarize the main points you've made ...

11 Asking for information about bills of exchange

Bank advisor:	Trade Finance. Can I help you?
Customer:	Hello, I'm calling from Capper Trading. We've just had a large export order – our first, in fact – and we're planning to use a bill of exchange or a bank draft. Unfortunately, I'm not at all clear about some of the conditions.
Bank advisor:	Well, perhaps I can clarify them for you. That's what I'm here for!
Customer:	OK. Your instructions talk about the drawer, the drawee and the payee. But aren't the drawer and the payee the same thing?
Bank advisor:	No. The drawer is the party that issues a bill of exchange, and the payee is the party to whom the bill is payable.
Customer:	Sorry, I don't quite follow you. Surely the bill is payable to us, as we're the seller?
Bank advisor:	Well, that depends whether you use a bank draft or a trade draft. A bank draft is payable to the bank. Unless you use a trade draft, issued by you.
Customer:	Er, could you go over that again, please?
Bank advisor:	If you use a bank draft, the buyer pays us, and then we pay the money to you, less any charges due to us. If you, the exporter, issue the bill, it's referred to as a trade draft, and it's payable to you.
Customer:	Oh, I see. And if you issue the bill, it's generally payable 30, 60 or 90 days from the bill of lading date, is that right?
Bank advisor:	Yes.
Customer:	What exactly does that mean?
Bank advisor:	The bill of lading is a document that the ship's master signs, acknowledging that the goods have been received for shipment, describing them, and giving details of where they are going. But of course you can always get the bill endorsed.
Customer:	Sorry, did you say 'endorsed'?
Bank advisor:	Yes, you can endorse it to the bank.
Customer:	Could you explain that in more detail?
Bank advisor:	Yes. We can endorse the bill before it matures. That means we guarantee to pay the bill if the buyer doesn't. Then you can sell it at a discount in the financial markets.
Customer:	I don't quite see what you mean.
Bank advisor:	It means you can get most of the money immediately, and you don't have to wait for the buyer to pay the bill. For example, you sell the bill at 99%, and the discount represents the interest the buyer could have received on their money until the bill's maturity date.
Customer:	Oh right. OK, thank you very much.
Bank advisor:	My pleasure. Goodbye.

12 Concluding a meeting

Chair: I'm sorry, John, but I'm afraid we'll have to bring this point to a close. I think we've covered everything, and it seems that we all agree on the way ahead, so I'd like to go over the decisions we've taken.

We're going ahead with the plan to redesign and refurbish some of our branches and to relocate the others. John is going to look into the question of finding more suitable premises for the branches in List B, possibly in shopping centres, and contact property agencies. Julie will contact the company that designed our most recent branches, and also investigate their main competitors in the refurbishment business. Remember, we need a company that specializes in banks because of the security aspects, and preferably one that can arrange to do the building work out-of-hours – in the evenings and at weekends – so that normal trading can continue. Alan, you're going to see if any more market research data is available about customer expectations. Claire, you're responsible for getting more information about what facilities the back office staff in the branches in List A would like from a major modernization or upgrading.

Is that all clear? Does everyone agree with that? Good. Kirsten, you'll let us have a copy of the minutes by when – Wednesday? Good, thank you. Can we fix a date for our next meeting? I expect we need about three weeks? Can we say Monday the twenty-second, at nine?

Well, thank you, everybody, it's been a very productive morning, and I look forward to our next meeting.

13 Freely floating exchange rates

Peter Sinclair: I think a lot of people would say that there's been an important trend towards more flexibility in exchange rates. So, for example, the pound now floats freely in terms of other currencies, the central bank doesn't intervene – only very, very rarely – and that's true for an increasing number of countries.

… the market system is now doing, say in the case of sterling, what central banks and finance ministries used to do in the past, which is trying to pick and stick to an appropriate level for the currency. But there are problems with the markets: markets are not perfect. One problem is that nobody knows the future and if there is an unexpected piece of news about a country, say you discover a vast amount of oil or the government suddenly falls and is likely to be replaced by one which has a very different financial, tax, or monetary policy, then everybody will suddenly wake up and say, 'Hey this is a country whose currency we must buy lots of' or 'This is now really unsafe, we must get out.' And the swings in exchange rates can be absolutely enormous, you can see a currency go up or down by one, two, three percent maybe in a day, in response to certain news.

… a lot of the people who are operating in foreign exchange markets don't tend to think so much about the long run and what the currency really ought to be worth in order for its goods to be priced at the right level in foreign markets and so on. They're trying to guess very short-term trends, and they're trying to guess the hunches of other traders. They tend to say, 'Oh, let's see, if something is going up today it will probably go up tomorrow.' They just go in one direction and you often get huge exchange rate swings, going on for maybe even years, certainly for weeks and months, which are pushing the currency away from what it really ought to be. This is a source of worry and it's undoubtedly happening and it's due to the fact that people don't have perfect information and often tend to say, 'Well, if he's doing this then he must know something I don't, I'd better copy him', and that can be a recipe for real trouble.

15   Market report

Reporter: In Tokyo today, the Nikkei 225 was firmer at eight thousand five hundred and sixty-nine point three three. Stocks around Europe also advanced this morning, following Friday's late surge on Wall Street, when the Dow-Jones gained eighty points. In Paris, the CAC-40 is up twenty points, although France Telecom plunged three euros fifty to thirteen fifty-five after the company issued a profit warning, and Thomson dropped one per cent to eighteen point thirty-four. The DAX in Frankfurt is also up, by thirty-six points, although Lufthansa tumbled four per cent to seven point fifteen. In London, the Footsie 100 has climbed to four thousand two hundred and twenty point one. British Energy jumped to five pounds twelve after they published their six-monthly results. Notable losers in London, however, include Vodafone, which slumped to one pound sixteen.

On the commodity markets, copper, which seemed to be going through the roof last week, is steady at seventy-nine point seven cents a pound. Gold has slipped to three hundred and sixty-two dollars an ounce, while silver is almost unchanged at four point forty-four.

16.1   Catering choices

Project Manager: So, any surprises?

HR manager: No, not really. Well, yes, actually – the response rate. It was extremely high. We sent the questionnaire to about 50% of the staff, and got nearly 3,200 responses – that's around 80%.

Project Manager: That's very good. So what do they want?

HR manager: Food! And lots of it! There's a clear demand for both a staff restaurant, serving hot and cold lunches, and for coffee and sandwich shops. Most respondents already working in departments with restaurants say they only eat out once a week, on average. But they also say they wouldn't choose the same lunch option every day. They clearly expect a building with 8,000 people working in it to provide them with several choices.

Project Manager: Well that's OK, isn't it? That's more or less what we're already planning.

HR manager: Yes, but there's also a significant demand for breakfast as well – both cooked breakfast and coffee and pastries. Though on the other hand around 30% said they were likely to bring in their own lunch most days, and would like fridges and microwaves near their offices.

Project Manager: That's fine – it still leaves over 5,000 people to feed. And breakfast is no problem once you have the staff and the facilities. At the moment we're thinking of an 850-seat restaurant, serving around 2,500 meals daily, about three-quarters at lunchtime. In fact it'll be one of the largest restaurants of its kind in the country. In the world even.

16.2   Health and leisure needs

Project Manager: OK, what was next?

HR manager: Well, after they've eaten they seem to want to sweat it off! Over 90% are in favour of a gym, especially the female respondents. They want rooms for a range of exercise classes (aerobics and yoga and things), as well as full gym equipment like weights and running machines. Less than 20% asked for squash or badminton courts, so I'm not sure we need to plan those, but – wait for it – about 50 people said they would like a swimming pool!

Project Manager: A swimming pool? Where do they think we're going to put that?

HR manager: Er ... on the roof!

Project Manager: Oh dear, I think we're going to have to disappoint 50 people! Now, tell me about medical and health care.

HR manager: Well, I was a bit surprised, but hardly anyone expects a diagnostic doctor service or dental

	treatment. Most people said they prefer to have only one doctor, and to get treatment near where they live. There were also concerns over patient confidentiality.
Project Manager:	Yes, that doesn't surprise me. Most people don't want their employer to have access to their medical records. I guess we'll simply abandon that idea.
HR manager:	Yet over 65% were in favour of a health clinic for things like travel advice and inoculations. And 8% want cycle parking and changing facilities. This is higher than we expected.
Project Manager:	These people who cycle in Manhattan – they amaze me. But we'll clearly have to do something about that. Eight per cent of 8,000 is a lot. Anything else?
HR manager:	Well, 200 people want their own space in an underground parking lot, even though we specifically said this isn't an option.
Project Manager:	I can understand that – I'd like one too! But like you say, we can't even think about that.
HR manager:	And about 100 people – I know that's not a lot – want a convenience store where they could get things like newspapers and magazines, candy, cans of soda and 'emergency' purchases like tissues and headache tablets. I guess 8,000 customers is enough for a store like that; they have them in hotels with much fewer people.
Project Manager:	True, but we're not building a hotel. Our people will be working and not shopping most of the day. Anything else?
HR manager:	Yes, the 'Do you have any other concerns?' question showed that there are a number of things the staff are worried about. Understandably, a lot of respondents voiced fears about a terrorist attack, and want a lot of information about evacuation arrangements and fire precautions. I think we'll have to send everybody a special booklet about this, explaining what the architects are doing.
Project Manager:	Yes, that's a good idea.
HR manager:	And a lot of people seem to be worried about the time it will take to move around within the building. Most of them have never worked in a forty-storey high-rise, and certainly not in one with so many people working in it. This building is going to take some getting used to.

17   The role of banks

Peter Sinclair:	Well, the role of the investment banks; yes, they're certainly big, important players in mergers and acquisitions, and yes, they may sometimes try and drum up business, but I think that no well-run firm will want to engage in this kind of activity unless they see merit in doing so. So it isn't all driven by the banks.
	What we do note – and that is really interesting – is that when a company goes for a takeover, tries to take over another, the thing that's most important is its share price, the share price of the company doing the takeover. So if the share prices do well – which they did in the 80s and 90s, most of the time – companies feel richer, their shares are more valuable, so they tend to go out on a buying spree and they will get advice from big investment banks and merchant banks about when to buy and what to buy. And the potential victim of a takeover bid will obviously want to get advice from another national institution about how to defend itself, assuming that's what it wants to do.
	So we've seen a lot of acquisitions and mergers, some friendly mergers and some contested takeovers, a lot of them happening in a strong stock market. In the early twenty-first century, so far, we have been seeing share prices slide a bit and so mergers and acquisitions are becoming less frequent and of course less valuable. The value of companies has fallen so the

value of the activity for the merchant banks, investment banks, has been slipping too. It is very much a cyclical phenomenon – boom for shares means more takeovers, slump for shares means less.

18.1   Conditional offers

Administrative Director:	OK, I'm going to be direct about this. We need your offices to use as conference rooms for meetings with customers. I'm sorry to say this, but they're much too nice for an IT department! So we're asking you to relocate to some offices we've rented across the street. Of course this is only temporary, as we're all moving to the new building in a year's time.
IT Manager:	And why can't you use the offices across the street as meeting rooms?
Administrative Director:	Because they're a bit small. And dark. Two of them don't actually have any windows.
IT person:	You must be joking. We couldn't agree to that. Why would we go there?
IT Manager:	No, wait a second. We would consider a temporary move on condition that we get much larger offices in the new building.
Administrative Director:	I'm afraid 'much larger' is out of the question. But we'd be happy to discuss the size of your offices in the new building as long as we can have your current offices before the end of the month.
IT Manager:	I'm afraid we can't accept that. Discussing the size will not be enough. I say 'much larger' because as you know we are understaffed. We would agree to move temporarily provided that we got the go-ahead to hire the software designer and the systems analyst we need. Who would obviously require offices.
Administrative Director:	Well, we could offer you two extra offices, so long as no other department objects, but as you know I can't make staffing decisions.
IT Manager:	I'm sorry, but we wouldn't consider moving now unless you can guarantee us both the staff and the space we need.
Administrative Director:	Well, I'd be willing to take your request to the next Board meeting if you agreed to move out on the 26th. What would you say to that?
IT Manager:	I'm afraid that still doesn't meet our requirements.

18.2   Should we grant this loan?

Sally:	So, Chris, the situation is this. Capper Trading has the exclusive rights to manufacture Moggles toys, to go with a new children's cartoon series on the television. I don't know if you've heard of it …
Chris:	No.
Sally:	Well it goes out every day, early in the evening, and the kids seem to love it, and the toys based on the series – they're little plastic figures – are selling really well. But Capper can only produce 20,000 a week. They don't want to take on extra staff and run two shifts in the factory, because they don't know how long these toys will go on selling. So they want to sub-contract to a company in China, and they want to start immediately. They have a company lined up, but they're going to have to pay them 60 days after the first shipment, and they don't have a big enough cash flow.
Chris:	OK, so how much cash do they currently have?
Sally:	Well, none. But that's because they're too successful! They've spent all their money on raw materials, and they're making these toys, and they're selling as fast as they can supply them, but the wholesalers haven't paid them yet, and they need to import more.

Chris:	Have they got firm orders for the toys they want to import from China?
Sally:	Yes. For 100,000 toys. But they're sure they'll soon get more orders, when the first ones sell out. They want to import 500,000.
Chris:	Yeah – and what happens if suddenly the series isn't popular any more or all the kids have got the toys, and your company - what are they called?
Sally:	Capper Trading.
Chris:	And Capper Trading has to pay for up to half a million toys they can't sell, that they've bought with our money?
Sally:	They don't think that's going to happen.
Chris:	Of course they don't. But it could, couldn't it? Look, bring them in, let's have a meeting tomorrow afternoon.

19   Derivatives

Peter Sinclair:	Derivatives are a very mysterious phenomenon. They are not entirely new but there has been an enormous growth in them recently, and what they are is funny kinds of financial trick which change the structure of risks and returns. Often they promise higher return on average but at the cost of big increase in risk, that's their usual property.
	OK, so who buys them and why are they undertaken? Sometimes people undertake financial derivative transactions actually to make themselves safer, to hedge. They've got a bill, let's say, coming up, which has to be paid in US dollars. Well, the sensible thing to do is try and hold some US dollar assets ahead so that if, when the day comes when you have to pay this US dollar bill, the dollar hasn't in the meantime gone up very sharply, which could spell real trouble for you. So hedging is actually an important source of demand for derivatives; and companies can, in appropriate circumstances, make their financial position much stronger and much safer by undertaking these activities. But these derivatives are complicated, they certainly may not be fully understood even by the banks which are rather keen on doing trades in them.
Steve Harrison:	You have to adopt a balanced view of derivatives, because they have had a very bad press. There have been some very well-cited examples of misuse of derivatives, and these have caused problems in the market – potentially they could have caused a lot of dislocation in various markets. But I think we need to recognize that derivatives have been around for a very long time, in various formats, and that used properly they can be a very helpful financial management tool. Derivatives can ensure that some of the unpredictability that occurs in the financial market is hedged, or neutralized, at least to some degree. However, if derivatives are misused, they have the capacity to cause a great deal of damage.
	Generally speaking, derivatives are used to protect certain positions, although they can also give you exposure to areas that the bank decides that it wants to have exposure to. With regard to speculation, I think it depends on the degree of speculation. Financial institutions are in the risk and reward business – to get the reward, they have to take a risk. So derivatives are another tool you can use to take risks – to expose yourself to risk in certain areas where you decide to do that.

20.1 Concluding an unsuccessful negotiation

Ajay Sharma: The major sticking point at the moment seems to be staff training. What exactly are your objections to our proposal?

Alice Hewlett: The problem is not with training so much as with staff retention. We are worried that the way the call centre industry is booming in India, and given the rapid staff turnover, our customers may be talking to people who are quite new to your company and who have not had enough training or experience with our products. We need some guarantees about the people who will be answering our customers.

Ajay Sharma: I think we both need to give a little ground here. What do you think is a reasonable solution?

Alice Hewlett: That you guarantee that all the employees answering our calls will have had at least three months' working experience with bank products.

Ajay Sharma: Well, I'm sorry, Mrs Hewlett, but we cannot do that. Perhaps we should adjourn to reconsider our positions? Hopefully we can come back with some fresh ideas.

Alice Hewlett: I'm sorry, but I don't think that would help. I've told you where we stand on this, and we can't change our position. And if you can't give us a guarantee on this, we'll have to look elsewhere. I'm afraid that we've reached a stalemate, so I think we should call it a day.

20.2 Concluding a successful negotiation

Representative of computer manufacturer: OK, we can agree to that. The option will run until the end of the year.

…

Can we just run through what's been agreed? We're going to deliver five hundred T650 workstations at $1,450 each, in fourteen days – which is to say, the twenty-third of May – with a payment period of 60 days. These workstations will be fully guaranteed for twelve months. And you have an option to buy two hundred more T650s at the same price until the end of the year.

…

I expect you'd like that in writing! We'll draw up a full contract. Well, I think we've both got a good deal. I hope this can be the basis for a long-term relationship.

20.3 Saturday opening

Employee A: I saw the top secret 'Saturday report' today. It's going to happen.

Employee B: Not without negotiations with the staff association, it's not. So what are they planning?

Employee A: I can't tell you. I told you – it's confidential!

Employee B: Oh, come on.

Employee A: Well, OK. I think they're sending round a circular tomorrow anyway. So, they're planning to open most branches on Saturdays, from ten till two, and to stay open an hour longer on weekdays.

Employee B: And they think they're going to find enough volunteers to work on Saturday?

Employee A: Oh no, not volunteers. They want to change all our contracts, though of course not everyone will have to work at the weekend. At least, not every weekend.

Employee B: I don't believe it! What are they offering in return?

Employee A: Two hours off – a two-hour reduction in the working week for all staff who work on Saturdays. Though the new branches will be so nice, people won't want to work less!

Employee B: You must be joking!

Employee A: I am joking. And they're going to create 25 new jobs, or 50 part-time ones. And there'll be an annual bonus for all staff if sales of banking products increase with the longer opening hours.

| Employee B: | Yeah, but what if there isn't any increase in business, and customers just come in at a different time? On Saturday instead of during the week. There'll be no bonuses. |
| Employee A: | They're convinced that won't happen. |

21.1   Asset management and allocation

| Paula Foley: | Asset management nowadays means managing financial assets – excluding real estate, works of art, and things like that. Individual portfolios and institutional funds are very different, because of size and objectives. There are many classes of possible investments in this area: bonds, stocks, cash, precious metals, funds and so on. Each of these classes contains a certain number, and sometimes a very large number, of sub-classes, like categories of bonds or international stocks of various countries. |

The problems for managing assets in this area concern, first of all, the objectives of the portfolio, of the client, and its size. The objectives of a private portfolio will depend on whether you invest for retirement or for use in the next few years, for instance to buy real estate. Another major factor is size, because you can easily diversify and then steer a large portfolio, and it is sometimes much more expensive to do so for a small one. This problem of objectives and portfolio diversification has a direct impact on the returns which are needed or expected to meet these objectives and the implied risk of these portfolios, a risk which depends largely on the returns that are expected.

In practice, the two major questions which arise are first, defining a strategy, and second, an investment style. The strategy in fact means asset allocation. You need to decide what proportion of the funds you will invest in those various classes: bonds, stocks and so on. The asset allocation is the key to the performance of the portfolio, whether it is between industries, between countries, or anything else. It is also the heart of the implementation of a reasonable diversification. But mind you, diversification can be overdone, and then it becomes a very expensive and unproductive exercise.

21.2   Investment styles

| Paula Foley: | The second point is style, which is very often not recognized by investors. There are a number of styles of investment management, the main ones being first of all, growth investment, which, as the word says, is looking for growth – for capital accumulation – and looks for growth companies in growth industries. The second is value, which is the opposite of growth, which is conservative industries with high asset values and stable or low-growing earnings. |

The third main style is the choice between large and small companies, on the equity side. Large companies are supposed to be stable and more reliable; small companies very often give a faster rate of growth, but are more difficult to track and manage.

Another point here is when you have invested your funds, you still have to manage your portfolio, which may take up to a year to build up. There are essentially two ways to manage a portfolio. One is active management, where you buy and sell quite frequently, to adapt your portfolio to your objectives, and to changing market circumstances. The other one is passive investment: you buy and hold, which used to be for many years, sitting on your positions, until things fundamentally changed or bonds came to maturity. This has now been developed into index-linked portfolios, which try to follow stock market or bond market indices, and replicate their movements. This can be a very attractive proposition, or not, considering that these portfolios go down with the market in negative times.

A final important remark is that portfolios which are composed of funds also need to be managed. You cannot buy and sit on a fund portfolio indefinitely. Funds change – they change their management, they change their quality and their objectives; therefore, just like an ordinary portfolio, a fund portfolio has to be managed too.

22   The introduction

Paula Foley: Good morning everybody. Thank you all for coming today. My name is Paula Foley, and I'm Vice-President for Private Banking. This morning I'm going to talk about conservative portfolio strategies, because most of you are responsible for an increasing number of clients who choose this option. My presentation will take about fifteen minutes, and as you can see, I've divided it into four parts. The first part will be about risk management in general. The second part looks at diversification, which is of course the most important concept of all. Then I'll talk about the use of indexed funds, and finally I'll discuss capital preservation and capital accumulation. If anything isn't clear, or if you have any questions, please don't hesitate to interrupt.

OK. So, what is risk management? ...

23.1   The Financial Services Authority

Steve Harrison: I think I'm correct in saying that the FSA came into existence on the first of June 1998. It was formed from nine organizations, I believe, although it may be slightly more now because extra responsibilities have been added to its mandate. The creation of the FSA was in recognition of developments taking place in the financial markets, the way firms were organizing themselves. The firms are not just banks any more, they're more like financial conglomerates, and so there needed to be a way to ensure that the supervision of these firms is appropriate.

The firms were becoming more and more integrated, and in order to make financial regulation more efficient, it was felt that the regulator in the United Kingdom should consider doing the same thing. So the decision was made to establish an integrated financial regulator incorporating all of those different elements.

When it's working with banks like ours, the FSA's main objective is to understand the institution, what it's currently doing and what it's seeking to do. The FSA is governed by statutory objectives such as protecting consumers and fighting financial crime. So that underpins all of its work. But the nature of its job, in relation to us, is to communicate with a wide range of people in the institution, both in our compliance department and at very senior executive levels. The FSA needs to understand our strategy as well as what we are doing on a day-to-day basis, in terms of our products and of how we are treating our customers. These customers may be consumers but they can also be what we would call wholesale counterparties – other banks that we deal with on a regular basis.

23.2   Conflicts of interest

Steve Harrison: ... We need to recognize that there have always been conflicts of interest. The crux of the problem is not the fact that we have them, but the way in which firms manage these conflicts of interest.

Often it's about how you control information within financial institutions. Increasingly, different parts of the firm will interact with the same counterparty, but in different ways. For example, there has been a situation in the press regarding equity research, where research analysts have been used almost to promote investment banking. That's caused a number of problems because retail investors – certainly in the USA – have purchased shares in firms on the basis of the research analysts' recommendation. There has been a suggestion that the view the analysts gave on those firms was actually not their real view. Their private view was that the firms were not nearly as attractive as they stated publicly, but they made these statements because there was a chance that if they did, then the firm would give investment banking work to the bank. Statistics in the UK show that the number of buy recommendations on firms substantially outweigh the number of sell recommendations on firms, so clearly there is a balance to be achieved here.

There's also auditing. Certainly a number of auditing firms have realized that the set of skills that they have within the firm means they are often very well placed – and legitimately placed – to provide extra consultancy-style work. Again, that is not necessarily a problem – what needs to be monitored is how this is managed with respect to the relationship with the client of the auditor. But certainly I think it's fair to say that many auditing firms have recognized this conflict in recent years and have either separated their consultancy business from the auditing firm, or have used other techniques to manage the potential conflict of interest. One of those has been, for example, that when they appoint an auditor, many clients now deliberately state that they will not use that firm for consultancy work. They will use another auditing firm for their consultancy work.

24.1 Parts of a presentation

Paula Foley: ... OK, so as I said, first of all I'm going to talk about financial futures, before moving on to options. As you probably know, futures were first traded on ...

... That's all I need to say about futures, so that completes the first part of my talk. Now let's turn to options, which are this department's specialty ...

... That's all I'm going to say about options, so unless you have any questions let's move on to the third part of my presentation, which is about swaps. As I said in my introduction, these fall into two main categories: interest rate swaps and exchange rate swaps. I'll begin with interest rate swaps, which some of you ...

... So that was interest rate swaps. Now we come to exchange rate swaps, which are still an important derivative instrument, even after the introduction of the euro ...

24.2 The end of a presentation

Paula Foley: OK, that's all I have to say about capital preservation and accumulation, so now I'll just summarize my three main points again. A conservatively managed portfolio should be widely diversified; it should be expected to rise or fall in line with one or more major stock indices; and it's more important to preserve capital than to accumulate it. So, to conclude, I have two recommendations. Firstly, I think we need to diversify our clients' portfolios more widely, probably across more than one stock market. And, secondly, given the current volatility of the markets, I think we all need to pay more attention to preserving our clients' initial capital sums than to increasing them.

Thank you all for your attention. Does anyone have any questions or comments?

Word list

Numbers shown are unit numbers, not page numbers.

A

abolish (verb)	1
acceptance	11
accountable	23
accounting	7
accounting methods	23
acquisition	17
active management	21
adjourn	20
advisable	23
advising bank	11
affluent	3
after-tax profit	7
agenda	10, 12
amendment	11
amenities	16
amortization	7
analyst	23
AOB (any other business)	10
apologies (for absence)	10
applicant	11
application	11
appreciate	13
asset allocation	21
asset management	21
assets	3, 7
asset-stripping	17
auditing	7
auditor	23
automatic deposit machine	6

B

balance	1, 3
balance sheet	7
bank account	1
bank charges	1
bank draft	11
banknote	9
bankruptcy	15
bar chart	22
base rate	9
bear	15
bear market	15, 21
beat the market	21
beneficiary	11
bill of exchange	11, 14

blue chip	15
bond	1, 5
bondholder	5
bonus	8
bookkeeping	7
boom	17
branch	3
brand name	7
bubble	15
building society	1
bull	15
bull market	15, 21
buying spree	17

C

call centre	10
call option	19
capital	1, 9, 15
capital accumulation	21, 24
capital preservation	21, 24
carriage	11
cash flow	5
central bank	1, 9
chair	10
chairman	10
checking account	5
cheque	3
collateral	5, 15
commercial bank	3, 5
commercial banking	3
commission	7
commodity	19
competition	17
compliance	23
comply	23
compromise (noun and verb)	10, 18
concession	18
conditional	18
conflict of interest	23
conglomerate	1, 17
consensus	10
conservative industry	21
consolidated	7
consultant	23
consulting	23